William R. Prince

Prince's Select Descriptive Catalogue

of the unrivaled collection of fruit & ornamental trees and shrubs, vines,

creepers

William R. Prince

Prince's Select Descriptive Catalogue
of the unrivaled collection of fruit & ornamental trees and shrubs, vines, creepers

ISBN/EAN: 9783337225292

Printed in Europe, USA, Canada, Australia, Japan

Cover: Foto ©Andreas Hilbeck / pixelio.de

More available books at **www.hansebooks.com**

WM. R. PRINCE & CO.

FLUSHING, NEAR NEW YORK.

------- *

ANNOUNCEMENT AND GENERAL REMARKS.

THE Senior Proprietor, Wm. R. Prince, having devoted more than half a century to Pomological and Horticultural pursuits, and desiring now to withdraw from all active business, has transferred the control of the Nurseries to his son, *William Prince*, who, with his associates, will conduct the establishment in its future operations. W. R. P. will, however, give his general supervision to some of the most prominent objects.

We need scarcely to announce that our Catalogues are not made up from books only, but that we possess in quantity, every article comprised in them. Many highly estimable *New Varieties* have been added to the present Catalogue, and we shall furnish descriptions of the New Fruits for the next edition of "*Downing's Fruit Trees;*" and we refer to his present and future editions for the identity of the Fruits in our collection. An additional plot of 40 acres of excellent Farm land, very favorably situated, has been added to the Nurseries, on which are now growing several hundred thousand trees, in addition to our previous extensive stock.

This and the other Nurseries are all on lands that may be termed *new soil* (in regard to Tree culture), no trees having been previously grown on them; as the building innovations have pressed upon our path so rapidly that the lands formerly occupied by our Nurseries are now populous streets, studded with dwellings. The natural strength and fertility of the soil of this locality is such, that it insures a most healthy and vigorous growth to the trees, which seem to become hardened and confirmed as they progress, and is devoid of that rank, stimulated, and unnatural exuberance which trees so generally exhibit when reared on lands that have never been subjected to previous culture. The Trees thus cultivated, after making at first a rapid development, are so sensitive to cold, that the winter easily affects them, and they gradually pine away till they become feeble and unproductive.

The climate of *Long Island* being subject at all times to the boisterous winds of the Ocean and the Sound, seems to be particularly favorable to perfecting the hardihood of Trees. The vacillations of alternate cold and mild periods during the winter, accompanied by the frequent freezings and thawings to which trees are here subject throughout all stages, prepares them for the endurance of the utmost degree of cold and rigor incident to the most northern latitude; it being found that trees, like men, become much more hardened in a changeable climate than in one regularly cold where the constitution is not subjected to trials.

It is doubtless from this cause that the Long Island Trees with which New England has been generally supplied, and also those which have been sent to the coolest regions of the West, have been found to better withstand the severest winters, than those which have been obtained from other localities. Indeed, it can be readily realized that trees so robust and hardy, and yet so vigorous, must possess a great superiority over those grown in localities where the mercury sinks each year to 10° and 20° below zero during a very prolonged winter, thus retaining the trees in a frozen, torpid and death-like state for many months, freezing and bursting the inner vessels, affecting the sap, and probably causing sap-blight, and weakening them to such a degree that they can never regain their original health and strength. Some lessons may be derived from the fatal experience of the three past winters at the West, to which may be superadded the inconsiderate use by many nurseries of unsuitable stocks for budding and grafting, and especially of the tender Mazzard stock for Cherries, instead of the hardy Mahaleb, the latter alone being suited to the North and West. No Trees grown here are ever winter-killed; and the pear-blight, so destructive in the western part of this State, is unknown here.

Our large General Catalogues, which have been distributed throughout the Union, comprise every estimable variety of Fruit ripening throughout the year, and especially such as have been recommended by the different Pomological Conventions, and embrace Trees of the usual sizes for planting in Orchards and Gardens. All are in the most healthy and vigorous state, and will be supplied at the rates named in the present Catalogue; and it may be taken as a rule that we will at all times sell as low, and many articles lower than they can be obtained elsewhere, *of equal size and quality. The Extra-Large sized Trees*, which are in a bearing state, have required many years to bring them to their present size, and *are such as can seldom be obtained elsewhere*, and are worthy of the special attention of those who desire *Fruit Trees for immediate bearing*, whereby many years are gained in the planting of Orchards and Gardens. The Extra-Large sized Ornamental Trees and Shrubbery, including the Large sized Evergreens, are worthy the particular attention of those who desire to promptly embellish their Lawns, Avenues, and other Grounds, and many of them are especially adapted to Cemeteries. None of the Apples and Pears, or other Fruit Trees, are grafted on pieces of roots, as has been inconsiderately practiced elsewhere.

Our collection of estimable Fruits of every class, and of Ornamental Trees and Shrubs, including Evergreens, is more general and extensive than any other in our country. We do not here, as is customary and necessary in the western Nurseries of our State, cover three-fourths of our grounds with Apple Trees and other common Fruits; but in accordance with the general demands of our Correspondents, we embrace an assortment very enlarged and comprehensive. It will consequently be seen that of Ornamental Trees and Flowering Shrubs, Evergreens, Roses, Climbers, Bulbous Flowers, and Herbaceous Flowering Plants of every Class, there is no comparison between the collections in the Flushing Nurseries and some distant ones, which have been unduly puffed *for their extent in acres*. Distant purchasers, and especially those located in the new and rising States of the North and West, should not allow themselves to be duped by gross misrepresentations emanating from interested sources, but should make it an indispensable duty to visit and inspect the Long Island Nurseries to their perfect satisfaction. We append hereto (on the cover) a list of the various Catalogues, which comprise all the departments of our Nurseries, each with prices annexed.

In consequence of the railroad which connects Flushing with the city of New York being laid 2,000 feet through one of our largest Nurseries of fifty acres, we will supply Nurseries and others requiring large numbers of Trees, at reduced rates, and on the most liberal terms, as that portion of our lands is required for building lots. We especially suggest to younger Nurseries the importance to them of securing genuine warranted Fruit Trees of our superior varieties, many of which are not obtainable elsewhere.

All trees, &c., are labeled and packed in a superior manner, in matted bales or boxes, so that it is scarcely possible that any can be injured; and we charge for the packing barely the actual cost. We feel assured that we save to purchasers more than ten per cent. by our superior packing, by which even the smallest articles go safely. The numbers on the trees and plants refer to the invoice and not to the Catalogues. We ship the packages, or send them by Railroad, by the Transportation Lines, or Express Lines, precisely as ordered; and we send the receipt for the packages with the invoice to the purchaser, and there is consequently the best security for their delivery. After being thus expedited by us, they are at the risk of the purchaser, and the forwarders alone are to be held responsible therefor. Remittances may be made by Check or Draft; but if Bank Notes are sent, they should be forwarded through the United States Express, American Express, or Adams' Express Co's., and the Agent's receipt therefor be sent to us. New York or Eastern Bank Notes are best, as there is a discount on Western notes.

Orders for Trees, &c.—Orders should be sent direct to us. It is indispensable that every order be plainly and regularly made out, naming the edition of the Catalogue selected from, and also that plain directions stating how the packages are to be marked and forwarded, should immediately follow the order, and *that these be entirely distinct from the letter.* It is also necessary to state in the orders for Fruit trees, whether Standards, Pyramids, or Dwarfs are wanted, and on what stock each kind is preferred. When any variation is allowed as to the precise kinds, by substituting others equally good or better, or when the selection of all or part of the varieties are left to us, we will exercise our judgment for the interest of the purchaser; and we cultivate none but the choicest varieties. If an error of any kind should occur, we desire to be promptly notified, that it may be rectified at once.

Specimen Trees.—Whenever specimen Trees are ordered by any Nurseryman or other person, they will be charged at the retail prices without discount, the extra time required to make such selections being important to us, and their accuracy of vital importance to the purchaser. As our desire is to sell Trees in quantities, we deem it a favor to supply specimen trees, and shall expect the purchaser to order at least two of each variety desired. In fact, many of the New and Rare Varieties are worth five times the price demanded, they having been obtained with great trouble and expense. We have never employed any Traveling Agents, and caution the public against some scoundrels who, having by some means obtained our Catalogues, profess to represent the Flushing Nurseries, and have repeatedly stated they were acting for us. If we should conclude to employ any Agents, their names will be announced in the Horticulturist; but we much prefer to do our own business by direct correspondence.

N. B. It seems almost superfluous to remark, that all the Trees and Shrubs in this Catalogue not stated to be tender, are hardy.

Steamers direct, and the Railroad Line, leave Fulton Market wharf, New York, hourly, for Flushing.

APPLES—PYRUS MALUS.

Standard Trees of usual size for Orchards, 25 cents.
" of larger size, 4 to 5 years grafted, 37 cts.
" very large, 6 and 7 years grafted, 50 cts.

N. B.—The two last-named sizes are such as are seldom obtainable from Nurseries.
Dwarf Trees, 25 to 37 cts., and extra size and age, 50 cts.

Above 400 varieties are cultivated, comprising every estimable variety described by Thomas, Downing, Manning, Barry, Kenrick, and Ives, and by the London Horticultural Society. The following comprise a selection of the most estimable, and we exclude a large number of worthless varieties which are comprised in many Catalogues.

Class 1.—SUMMER VARIETIES.

1 Benoni, *very fine.*
2 Belle d'Aout, 50 cts.
3 Blinkbonny, *very fine*, 50 cts.
4 Buffington Early.
5 Corse's Favorite, *fine*, 50 cts.
6 Early Harvest.
7 Early Joe.
9 Early Strawberry.
10 Garretson's Early, *very fine.*
11 Golden Sweet.
12 Keswick Codlin.
13 Large Yellow Bough.
14 Lyman's Large Summer.
15 Primate (*true*).
17 Red and Green Sweet (*monstrous*).
18 Red Astrachan.
19 Sinequanon.
20 Summer Bellflower.
21 Summer Hagloe.
22 Summer Pearmain (*Amer*).
23 Summer Queen.
24 Summer Rose.
25 Summer Russet.
25½ Summer Spitzemburgh.
26 Summer Sweet Paradise.
26½ Williams' Favorite.
27 William Prince. (*Lond. Hort. Soc.*)

Class 2.—AUTUMN VARIETIES.

28 Autumn Bough—Fall Bough
29 Late or Autumn Strawberry.
31 Beauty of the West.
34 Boxford.
35 Cooper (Ohio).
36 Doctor, or De Witt.
37 Drap d'Or—Orange Pippin.
38 Fall Pippin.
39 Gravenstein.
40 Hawley—Dowse.
41 Holland Pippin.
43 Lindley's Nonpareil (Southern).
44 Lowell.
45 Lyscom.
46 Maiden's Blush.
47 Monstrous Bellflower.
48 Nyack Pippin.
49 Pomwater Sweet, *finest baking.*
51 Pearmain, Gardener's Sweet.
52 Pearmain, Scarlet.
54 Dyer—Pomme royale.
55 Porter.
57 Princeall.
58 Pumpkin Russet (Sweet R't.)
59 Rambo.
60 Scarlet Nonpareil.
60½ Sum'r Pippin—Sour Bough.
61 St. Lawrence.
62 Sweet, Haskell.
63 Sweet, Jersey.
64 Sweet, Pumpkin, Lyman's Pound Sweet.
65 Sweet, Peach Pond.
66 Sweet, Rams lell's.
67 Sweet, Willis, *fine baking.*
68 Sweet, Superb.

Class 3.—WINTER VARIETIES.

70 American Golden Russet.
71 Bailey Sweet.
72 Baldwin.
74 Bellefleur, Yellow.
76 Belmont.
78 Broadwell.
79 Carthouse, *Gilpin. Red Romanite, of Ohio.*
80 Chandler.
81 Cogswell.
82 Cumberland Spice.
83 Dickskill.
84 Domine.
86 Dutch Mignonne.
88 Fallawater.
89 Pomme de Neige.
90 Red Miami.
91 Golden Ball—Belle et bonne
92 Gooseberry, 50 cts.
92½ Henrick Sweet — Sweet Pearmain.
93 Hubbardston Nonsuch.
94 Jonathan.
95 King (*Tompkins County*).
96 Lady—Pomme d'Api.
96½ Laquier.
97 Maclean's Favorite.
98 Marston's Red Winter.
99 McLellan.
100 Melon.
101 Middle, or Mittle, *extra.*
102 Minister.
103 Mother.
104 Murphy.
105 Newark King.
106 Northern Spy.
108 Ortley, *Jersey Greening. White Bellefleur.*
109 Pearmain, Blue.
111 Pearmain, Herefordshire.
113 Pearmain, Winter.
Autumn Pearmain, Downing.
114 Peck's Pleasant, *fine variety of Newtown Pippin.*
115 Pennington Seedling.
118 Pippin, American Golden.
119 Pippin, Cranberry.
120 Pippin, Easter — French Crab.
122 Pippin, Monmouth.
124 Pippin, Green Newtown.
125 Pippin, Yellow Newtown.
126 Pippin, Red Sweet.
127 Pippin, Ribston.
128 Pippin, Springhill, *fine variety of Newtown pippin*, 50 cents.
130 Pomme de Lettre (keeps a year), 50 cts.
131 Pomme Grise (Russet,)
133 Prince's Yellow Winter, 50 cts.
134 Prior's Red.
135 Rawle's Janet.
136 Reinette de Caux, 50 cts.
137 Reinette, Canada.
138 Rhode Island Greening.
139 Roman Stem.

140 Rome Beauty (Ohio)—*Gillett's Seedling.*	151 Spitzemburgh, Flushing.	161 Sweet, Ladies.
141 Russet, Boston or Roxbury.	152 Spitzemburgh, Newtown.	162 Sweet, Seaver.
142 Russet, English (Downing).	153 Spitzemburgh, Springhill, *new variety of Esopus Spitzemburgh,* 50 cts.	163 Sweet, Talman.
143 Russet, Golden (English).		164 Sweet, Wells.
144 Russet, Honey.	154 Swaar.	165 Tewksbury Blush.
145 Russet, Imperial, *monstrous.*	155 Smokehouse.	166 Twenty Ounce (Pearmain).
146 Russet Pearmain.	156 Sweet, Danvers Winter.	167 Vanderveer.
147 Seeknofurther, Green.	157 Sweet, Green.	168 Victuals and Drink.
148 Smith's Cider (Table),	158 Sweet, Hartford.	169 Wagener.
149 Seeknofurther, Westfield.	159 Sweet, Phillip's.	170 Wine.
150 Spitzemburgh, Esopus.	160 Sweet, Lovett's.	171 Winesap.
		172 Winter Strawberry.

Class 4.—FOR PRESERVES AND ORNAMENT.

35 cts., except those noted.

173 Api étoilé, or Starry Lady Apple, 50 cts.	177 Siberian Small Red Crab.	183 Chinese Double White, 50 cents.
174 Manning's Siberian Red Crab, 50 cents.	178 Siberian Large Yellow Crab.	184 Rivers' Double Flowering, 50 cts.
175 Montreal Beauty Crab, 50 cents.	180 Power's Siberian Crab.	185 Prince's Roseate Double, *new,* 50 cts.
176 Siberian Large Red Crab.	181 Transcendent Crab, finest of all, 50 cts.	
	182 Chinese Double Red Flowering.	

VARIETIES OF APPLES RECENTLY ADDED TO OUR COLLECTION.

Bank Sweet.	Early Pennock.	Northern Greening, *long keeping.*
Bohannan.	Equinetely.	
Buckingham.	Fall Seeknofurther.	Oconee Greening.
Campfield.	Fulton.	Prolific Sweet.
Carolina Red June.	Genesee Chief.	Reinette Blanche d'Espagne.
Crab, Blood Red.	Hall.	Richard's Graft.
Crab, Currant.	Horse.	Seneca Favorite.
Crab, Hybrid.	Hubbardston Pippin.	Snediker.
Crab, Large Scarlet.	Indian Rareripe.	Superb.
Crab, Savannah.	Klaproth.	White Spitzemburgh.
Crab, Siberian Purple.	Lacker.	White Winter Pearmain.
Crab, Siberian Striped.	Limber Twig.	Winter Sweet Paradise.
Crab, White.	Mangum.	Winter Sweet Pearmain.
Crowser (Pennsylvania).	Maiden's Favorite.	Wood's Sweet.

Cider Apples.—Harrison and other Estimable Varieties can be supplied.

Rejected Apples.—The American Pomological Society have published a list of 125 Rejected Varieties, many of which are still offered for sale in some Nursery Catalogues. Purchasers should look well to this important point.

SELECT APPLES.

Class I.—SUMMER APPLES.

Benoni, medium size, roundish, deep red, striped, flesh yellow, tender, subacid, rich flavor, good bearer. Aug.

Blinkbonny, medium size, oblate, pale straw color, acid, spicy, the finest flavored of all early apples, productive, a great acquisition. Aug.

Corse's Favorite, medium, oblate, pale yellowish green, tender, very sprightly, subacid, unequalled in flavor for cooking, very productive, ripens gradually through August. A favorite fruit of Lower Canada.

Early Harvest, medium size, roundish oblate, pale yellow, tender, acid, rich, fine, ripens in succession, of slow growth, with slender shoots, but very productive. End of July and Aug.

Early Joe, rather small, oblate, deep red, tender, subacid, spicy, excellent, very productive. Last of Aug.

Early Strawberry, rather small, roundish, deep red, faint stripes, tender, subacid, pleasant, productive. Middle to end of Aug.

Garretson's Early, rather large, roundish, oblate, yellow, tender, subacid, rich, excellent, productive, a great acquisition. Aug.

Golden Sweet, large, roundish, pale yellow, sweet, good, fair, vigorous, productive. Late in Aug.

Keswick Codlin, rather large, conical, pale yellow, pleasant acid, juicy, good, excellent for cooking, very productive. Late in Aug.

Large Yellow Bough, or Early Bough, large, roundish, greenish yellow, sweet, very tender, excellent flavor, regularly productive. Aug.

Lyman's Large Summer, large, roundish, pale yellow, subacid, high flavor; a moderate bearer until the tree becomes large. Aug.

Priluate, medium size, pale yellow, with a blush, tender, mild and good flavor, vigorous, productive. Aug. and Sept.

Red Astrachan, large, roundish, oblate, bright crimson, beautiful, crisp, acid, juicy, good; vigorous, productive. Aug.

Sineqnauon, medium size, pale greenish yellow, tender, spicy, high flavored, excellent, grows slow and slender, productive. Aug.

Summer Pearmain, American, medium size, oblong, striped and dotted with red, tender, subacid, high flavored, excellent, ripening for several weeks; growth slow, very productive. Throughout Aug.

Summer Queen, rather large, conical, yellow striped with red, handsome, flesh yellow, subacid, rich, spicy, fine flavor, fine for cooking, vigorous growth. Aug.

Summer Rose, medium size, roundish oblate, yellowish blotched with red, very tender, crisp, juicy, mild subacid, excellent; grows rather slow, productive. Middle to end of Aug.

Williams' Favorite, medium size, oblong, crimson striped, mild, agreeable, moderately juicy, excellent, handsome, of moderate growth, productive. Ripens in succession during Aug.

Class II.—AUTUMN APPLES.

Late, or Autumn Strawberry, medium size, roundish, tender, juicy, agreeable subacid flavor, estimable, vigorous, and productive. Sept., Oct., and Nov.

Autumn Bough, medium or rather large, roundish, whitish, sweet, pleasant flavor, much esteemed, very productive. Sept.

Cooper (of Ohio), rather large, round oblate, greenish yellow, striped with red, crisp, juicy, pleasant, not high flavor, productive, much esteemed in Ohio. Midautumn.

Drap d'or, or Orange Pippin, large, roundish, golden yellow, showy, mild subacid, agreeable, moderately vigorous, productive. Sept. and Oct.

Fall Pippin, very large, roundish, rich yellow when ripe, flesh yellowish, rather firm, tender at maturity, rich, aromatic, excellent, vigorous, productive, greatly esteemed. Oct. to Dec.

Pomme de Neige, medium size, round, red, flesh very white, subacid, juicy, spicy, pleasant, much esteemed at the North, vigorous, a French variety, and also well known in Lower Canada. Oct. and Nov.

Gravenstein, rather large, roundish, yellow striped red, tender, juicy, subacid, rich, high flavored, excellent, handsome, vigorous, very productive, well suited to the North. Sept. and Oct.

Hawley, or Dowse, quite large, roundish, pale yellow, tender, fine grained, mild, rich fine subacid flavor, very valuable, rather slow growth, productive. Midautumn.

Holland Pippin; this is not the Summer Pippin, as is erroneously stated in some catalogues, but is an autumnal fruit totally distinct; very large, roundish, somewhat oblong, pale yellow, dull red cheek, flesh white, rather acid, secondary flavor, rigorous growth. Oct. and Nov.

Jersey Sweeting, medium size, round ovate, greenish yellow, striped with red, tender, juicy, very sweet, popular for table and cooking, vigorous, and productive. Sept. and Oct.

Lowell, or Orange, large, roundish oblong, fair, rich yellow, rather coarse, rich acid, excellent, vigorous, productive, finest of its period, and early bearer. It may be a synonym. Sept.

Lyscom, large, round, pale red stripes on yellowish ground, fine grained, mild subacid, moderately rich flavor, good second rate. Oct. and Nov.

Maiden's Blush, rather large, oblate, regular form, fair, pale yellow, red shaded cheek, beautiful, tender, pleasant subacid, good second rate, very productive. Midautumn.

Porter, rather large, oblong conical, bright yellow, fair, tender, rich subacid, fine flavor, a good Northern fruit, productive. Sept.

Dyer, or Pomme Royale, rather large, roundish, pale yellow, tender, very fine grained, very juicy, rich acid flavor, excellent, equaled by few, productive. Sept., Oct., and Nov.

Pumpkin Russet, or Sweet Russet, very large, round, slightly flattened, yellowish green russet, sweet, rich flavor, esteemed, vigorous growth. Oct. and Nov.

Rambo, medium, oblate, streaked and marbled yellow and red, tender, mild subacid, rich, juicy, fine flavor, vigorous growth, productive much esteemed everywhere. Oct. to Dec. at the North, but autumnal at the South.

Ramsdell's Sweet, very beautiful, sweet, excellent, productive.

St. Lawrence, large, roundish, dark red stripes on greenish yellow, rather acid, somewhat rich, agreeable, handsome, productive, a popular Canadian fruit. Midautumn.

Class III.—WINTER APPLES.

Bailey Sweet, large, ovate, bright red, beautiful, tender, mild, rich sweet, excellent, vigorous, upright growth. Nov. to Jan.

Baldwin, large, roundish, bright red striped and shaded on yellow ground, crisp, mild, rich, subacid flavor, handsome, vigorous and rapid upright growth, very productive. A first rate winter-keeping apple, and very suitable in connection with the Newtown Pippin for exportation; ripens throughout the winter.

Belmont, or Gate, rather large, ovate, pale yellow with a blush, flesh firm, crisp, becomes tender, mild, rich, subacid, fine flavor, very productive, highly valued in some of the Western States. Dec. and Jan.

Blue Pearmain, large, roundish, with dull purplish red stripes, a conspicuous bloom, flesh yellowish, mild, subacid, good, of slow growth, and produces only a thin crop. Oct. to Jan. The Flushing Spitzemberg much resembles it, and is a much more valuable variety.

Danver's Winter Sweet, medium size, roundish, yellow with sometimes a blush, flesh yellow, sweet, rich, tender, vigorous, and productive. Nov. to Mar.

Dutch Mignonne, quite large, roundish, orange with faint stripes, beautiful, firm flesh, becomes tender, rich, subacid, high flavor, rather coarse, growth erect, productive. Nov. to May.

Gooseberry, large, roundish oblate, yellow, sprightly, acid, peculiar flavor, first quality, a favorite London cooking fruit. Jan. to May.

Green Sweet, medium size, roundish, fair, greenish, very sweet, tender, spicy flavor, productive, and a long keeper, growth moderate. Nov. to May.

Hubbardston Nonsuch, large, roundish, ovate, yellow ground striped and dotted with light red, flesh yellow, tender, juicy, very rich, slightly subacid, blended with a rich, sweet, and excellent flavor, superior to the Baldwin in flavor, vigorous growth, very productive. Nov. to Jan.

Jonathan, medium size, round ovate, striped with bright red on yellow, very juicy, subacid, spicy, moderately rich, always fair and handsome, assimilating to the Spitzemberg character, shoots slender and divergent, very productive. Nov. to April.

Laquier, rather large, oblate, striped red on greenish yellow, flesh fine grained, firm, crisp, agreeable, mild subacid. Dec. to March.

Lady Apple, or Pomme d'Api, quite small, flat uniform, brilliant deep red cheek on light yellow flesh tender, crisp, juicy, mild, slight subacid good flavor, a beautiful fancy apple for parties, commands twice the price of any other apple; growth vigorous but not rapid, forms a beautiful regular conical tree with luxuriant foliage, some trees near Flushing have attained the height of 50 feet, each yielding 9 to 11 barrels. There is no variety of apples, large or small, that produces greater crops. Nov. to May.

Melon (Norton's), large, roundish, pale yellow with bright-red stripes and dots, flesh white, tender, subacid, spicy, very juicy, fine flavored, an excellent and beautiful fruit, of slow growth, productive. Nov. to Feb.

Middle, or Mittle, or Middel Apple, it is of very fine quality, very productive, and grew at a division fence, whence its name.

Minister, large oblong conical, striped red on pale yellow, flesh yellowish, subacid, moderately rich, second rate, fair and showy, vigorous growth, very productive. Nov. to Jan.

Monmouth Pippin, rather large, yellow with a bright red cheek, tender, juicy, fine flavor, vigorous and productive, a very estimable winter fruit. Dec. to April.

Mother, large ovate, rich red, flesh yellow, mild subacid and mixed with sweet, rich, very aromatic, somewhat juicy, very productive. It is well suited to the North. Nov. to Jan.

Northern Spy, large, roundish oblate, often flattened, red striped, dark crimson on the sun

side with a delicate bloom, beautiful, flesh juicy, rich, highly aromatic and retains freshness of flavor until late in the spring, a highly estimable fruit and suitable for exportation; growth very vigorous and erect, very productive. Leaves and fruit buds open late, thereby rendering it very suitable to the North. Dec. to June.

Pearmain, Herefordshire, we do not believe that more than one Nursery besides our own in the whole Union possesses this genuine variety; and that one obtained it from us. They all appear to have confused the common Winter Pearmain with this; and even Mr. J. J. Thomas, whom we deem a generally reliable author on Apples, has fallen into the same error. It is a much larger fruit than the Winter Pearmain, form oblong ovate, with dull red stripes on a pale greenish ground, flesh pleasant, sprightly acid, aromatic, juicy, tender, fine grained, high and pleasant flavor, will keep a month longer than the other variety, and is much the most valuable, productive. Nov. to March.

Peck's Pleasant, large, roundish, fair, pale yellow, with a brown cheek, flesh firm, very tender, mild, rich, clear subacid, fine Newtown Pippin flavor, a very estimable variety. Nov. to April.

Pennington Seedling, medium size, oblate, yellowish russet, flesh yellow, firm, crisp, brisk acid, high flavored, excellent, first quality. Dec. to March.

Pippin, Green Newtown, full medium and occasionally large, roundish oblate or flattened, dull green, becoming yellowish green, often dotted, with a brownish red cheek, flesh white, firm, crisp, fine grained, juicy, with a high aromatic flavor, unsurpassed in excellence, keeps long and preserves its freshness; growth rather slow, but quite equal to many other varieties, *rough bark* after the second year's growth. Immense quantities are grown on Long Island, and on the Hudson River, and it will doubtless succeed in any Apple region, on good free soil, with proper culture. Quantities of the finest fruit come from Western New York. Nurserymen have prejudiced purchasers against this tree, because its slower growth renders it less profitable to them than the rapid-growing varieties.

Pippin, Yellow Newtown. Scarcely any Nursery on this Island or elsewhere in the State possesses this very distinct and genuine variety; but many sell the preceding under the two distinct names of green and yellow, and have thereby caused the confusion as to identity. It is found disseminated in orchards to which we have supplied the true variety during the last 60 years. The fruit is rather large, more flattened than the preceding, clear light yellow, with a bright red cheek, fairer and handsomer, possessing the same qualities, but not quite equal in flavor, keeps during the same period, and is also suitable for exportation. The tree has a more thrifty appearance and grows faster than the preceding. This in Virginia is called "Albemarle Pippin."

Pippin, Ribston, medium or rather large, roundish, yellow and red, flesh yellow, crisp, juicy, very rich, sprightly acid flavor, productive. Succeeds well in the most northern localities, where it is a winter fruit, but it matures here in Oct. and Nov., and is also valueless.

Pippin, Springhill, a seedling of the Green Newtown Pippin, grown by Judge B. W. Strong, seems identical in character with the parent, and of equal excellence. It has proved of more thrifty growth.

Pomme Grise, small, roundish, gray russet, very tender, fine grained, rich, high flavor, good for dessert and cooking; the tree productive, well suited to the North, and a favorite in Canada. It is an old European variety.

Prince's Yellow Winter, medium, or rather large, roundish oblate, pale yellow, tender, juicy, fine flavor, a very estimable variety. Nov. to April.

Rawles Janet (Neverfail), medium size, roundish, conical, striped pale red on light yellow, firm, crisp, juicy, rich, mild subacid, fine grained, first quality, slow growth, very productive. Keeps very long, and is highly esteemed at the South and Southwest.

Reinette, Canada, quite large, flattened, greenish yellow, often a brown cheek, flesh firm, becomes tender, juicy, rich, sprightly subacid, vigorous growth, productive. It is a French variety, and succeeds well in Canada. Nov. to March.

Rhode Island Greening, large, roundish oblate, greenish yellow, fair and handsome, with a dull blush cheek, flesh yellow, subacid, tender, juicy, very pleasant, excellent for table and cooking; strong oblique growth, spreading, very productive; a most valuable market fruit. Nov. to March at the North, but a fall apple at the South.

Rome Beauty (of Ohio), very large, beautiful, roundish, bright red on pale yellow ground, flesh yellow, crisp, mild, subacid, juicy. Oct. to Dec.

Russet, Boston, or Roxbury, rather large, roundish oblate, rough russet on yellowish ground, often a dull brown cheek, flesh coarse, rather crisp, good subacid, not high flavor; growth vigorous and spreading, very productive. Nov. to June.

Russet Poughkeepsie, erroneously called by some "English Russet," small, roundish, ovate, brownish russet, flesh firm, subacid, aromatic flavor; very productive, and keeps till July or longer. It is probably of foreign origin, but very distinct from and much smaller than the following.

Russet, English Golden, medium size, roundish oblate, yellowish russet, fair and handsome, flesh firm, crisp, tender, rich, aromatic, juicy, estimable growth, vigorous, productive. Nov. to Mar.

Seeknofurther, Westfield, medium to large, roundish, fair, striped with dull red, partially russeted, flesh tender, spicy, rich, fine flavor, growth vigorous, productive. Succeeds well at the North and in Ohio. Nov. to Feb.

Seeknofurther, Green, medium size, roundish oblate, greenish yellow, flesh fine grained, subacid, juicy, very agreeable flavor. Nov. to Mar.

Spitzemburgh, Esopus, rather large, ovate, bright red, flesh yellow, firm, crisp, very aromatic, rich, subacid, unequaled in high flavor; growth slow, rather slender, moderate bearer, esteemed among the very best. Nov. to Mar.

Spitzemburgh, Flushing, large, round, conical, dark red, with white dots, and a thin bloom, flesh white, nearly sweet, aromatic, pleasant, good second-rate flavor, growth very vigorous, dense luxuriant foliage, moderately productive. Nov. to April.

Spitzemburgh, Springhill, a beautiful seedling of Esopus Spitzemberg grown by Judge B. W. Strong, medium size, ovate, bright red, flesh subacid, aromatic, rich flavor, estimable. Nov. to Mar.

Swaar, rather large, roundish, often oblate, pale lemon yellow, flesh yellowish, firm, fine grained, tender, spicy, slight subacid, mild, very rich, esteemed one of the best, growth moderate, very productive. Nov. to May.

Talman Sweeting, medium size, roundish oblate, whitish yellow, flesh white, firm, very sweet, secondary flavor for dessert, excellent for cooking; growth vigorous, very productive. Nov. to April.

Tewksbury Blush, small, round oblate, yellow with red cheek, flesh yellow, firm, juicy, good flavor, vigorous growth, very productive, keeps till July. It requires a long season to mature, and is therefore best suited to the South.

Twenty Ounce (Pearmain), very large, fair, and very beautiful, roundish oblate, striped rich red on yellowish ground, a monstrous Pearmain variety, flesh rather coarse, subacid, assimilating in flavor to the winter Pearmain, second rate, excellent for cooking. growth upright, productive. Popular at market, Oct. to Jan.

Vanderveer, usually misspelt "Vandervere," medium size, round oblate, pale red stripes on yellow ground, deep red on sunside, flesh light yellow, mild, subacid, rich, excellent flavor, growth fair, good bearer, does best on light soils. Oct. to Mar.

Wagener, medium to large, oblate, yellow striped pale red, deep red on sunside, flesh yellowish, aromatic, excellent, very productive. Dec. to May.

Winter Pearmain—Autumn Pearmain of Downing, medium or under, ovate, ends flattened, stripes of dull red on pale yellow, flesh dull yellow, very tender, subacid, aromatic, very pleasant, high flavored, growth moderate, very productive. An old and universal favorite. Nov. to Mar.

Yellow Bellflower, or Bellefleur, large, often very large, oblong ovate, yellow, with a blush cheek, flesh fine grained, very tender, subacid, crisp, juicy, sprightly aromatic, excellent, a splendid and favorite fruit, growth vigorous, very productive. Well adapted to the Northern and Middle States, and as far west as Kentucky. Nov. to April.

PEARS—PYRUS COMMUNIS.

Note.—There is never any *Pear Blight* or *Sap Blight* on Long Island, and the Trees are never injured by the winter.

The stock of Pears is the finest in the Union, and the prices low for the quality, and we can supply the leading and most esteemed varieties on both Pear and Quince. Such as do not succeed on the Pear we can supply on the Quince, and contrarywise.

Standards on Seedling Pear stocks, 3 to 4 years budded, . . 50 cts.
Do   do   extra size, 4 to 6 years, . 75 cts. to $1 50
Do   do   largest size, 8 and 9 years bearing age, 2 00
Pyramids and Dwarfs on Angers Quince, 3 years, . . . 50
Do   do   do   do   4 to 8 years, in full bearing, 75 cts. to 1 50
   according to age and size.
Secondary sized Trees to those priced at 50 cts. will be supplied at 37½ cts.
☞ The Extra Large sized Trees are suitable for prompt bearing, and seldom obtainable, and are usually sold at $3 to $5 each.
The American varieties are denoted by an asterisk. *

SUMMER VARIETIES.

2 Bartlett.
3 Beau present d'Artois.
4 Beurre Benoist.
5 Beure Giffard.
6 *Bloodgood (*slow growth.*)
7 *Brandywine.
8 *Canandaigua (Catharine.)
10 *Dearborn's Seedling (*slow growth.*)
11 Diller.
12 Doyenne d'été.
13 Duchesse de Berry d'été.
14 Elizabeth (Manning.)

15 Fondante agréable.
16 *Heathcot.
17 *Henrietta (Edwards.)
19 Honey, European.
20 *Hosea Schenck.
21 Jargonelle, English.
22 *Kingsessing.
23 Madeleine.
24 *Moyamensing,
25 *Muscadine.
26 *Osband's Summer.
27 *Ott.

28 *Prince's Sugar (not Sugar top.)
29 *Queen of August (*extra*), $1.
30 Rhenish Colmar, *very spicy,* $1.
   Summer Seckel.
31 Rostiezer.
32 Rousselet hatif.
35 Sugartop.
36 Summer Francreal.
39 Supreme de Quimper.
40 *Tyson.
41 *Williams' early.

AUTUMN VARIETIES.

42 *Abbott.
43 Alpha.
44 *Adams.
45 Ananas d'été.
46 *Andrews.
47 Baronne de Melo.
48 Belle Heloise (*distinct.*)
49 Belle Epine Dumas.
50 Belle Lucrative, see Fondante d'Automne.
51 Bergamotte Cadette.
52 Bergamot, Gansell's.
53 Bergamot, Oakley Park.
54 Bergamot, Platt's.
   Church or Clark.
55 *Bergen, Extra.
56 Beurré Bachelier.
57 Beurré Bosc (*slow growth.*)
58 Beurré, Brown.
59 Beurré Clairgeau.
60 Beurré de Brignais—Des Nonnes.
61 Beurré d'Anjou.
62 Beurré d'Amanlis.
63 Beurré d'Amanlis panaché.
64 Beurré de Koning.
65 Beurré Diel.
66 Beurré Duval.
67 Beurré, Golden Bilboa.
68 Beurré Hardy.
   Beurré Sterckmans.
69 Beurré de Montgeron.

70 Beurré Kossuth.
71 Beurré Moiret.
72 Beurré de Nantes.
73 *Beurré Preble.
74 Beurré Superfin.
75 Beurré Van Marum.
76 Bezi de la Motte.
77 Bezi de Montigny.
78 *Bleeker's Meadow.
   Large Seckel.
79 Bon chretien fondante.
80 *Buffum.
81 *Cabot.
82 *Calhoun, (Edwards)
83 *Capsheaf.
84 Catinka.
85 *Chapman.
86 *Citron (Edwards.)
87 *Collins.
88 Colmar d'Aremberg.
89 Colmar Van Mons.
   Surpasse Virgalieu.
90 Compte de Lamy.
91 Compte de Paris.
92 Conseiller de la Cour.
   Duc d'Orleans.
93 *Cushing.
94 *Dallas.
95 De Louvain.
96 Delices d'Hardempont d'Angers.
97 Delices de Jodoigne.

98 *Dikeman.
99 *Dix.
100 Doyen Dillen.
101 Doyenné Boussoch.
102 Doyenné Defais.
103 Doyenné, Gray.
104 Doyenné Robin.
119 Doyenné Rose.
120 Doyenné Sieulle.
121 Doyenné, White.
   Virgalieu.
122 Duc de Brabant.
123 Duchesse d'Angouleme.
124 Duchesse d'Orleans.
   Beurré St. Nicholas.
124 Dundas.
125 Dunmore.
126 *Early York.
127 *Edwards.
128 *Elizabeth (Edwards.)
129 Emile d'Hyest.
132 Figue d'Alençon.
133 Flemish Beauty.
135 Fondante d'Automne.
   Belle Lucrative.
136 Fondante Van Mons.
137 Fondante de Malines.
138 Forelle.
139 Frederic de Wurtemberg.
140 *Frederika Bremer.
141 *Fulton.
142 *General Taylor.

145 Graslin.	171 Nouveau Poiteau.	191 *Seckel (*slow growth.*)
147 *Hageman, *extra fine*, $1.	172 *Onondaga — Swan's Orange.	192 Serrurier.
148 *Harvard.		193 *Shelden.
149 *Henry (Edwards.)	173 *Ontario.	194 *Sheppard.
150 Henry VI.	174 *Oswego Beurré.	195 St. Ghislain.
151 *Howell.	175 *Oswego Incomparable.	196 St. Michael Archange.
152 *Hull.	176 Paradise d'Automne.	197 *Stansel.
153 Jalousie de Fontenay.	177 Paquency.	198 *Stephen's Genesee.
154 Jersey Gracioli.	178 *Parsonage.	199 *Sterling.
155 *Johonnot.	178½ *Petre.	201 *Ten.
156 *Jones' Seedling.	179 Pius IX.	202 Theodore Van Mons.
157 *Kirtland.	179½ *Philadelphia.	203 Thompson.
158 *Knight's Seedling.	180 *Pinneo or Boston.	204 Urbaniste.
159 Late Green Chisel.	181 *Pocahontas.	205 Van Assche.
Huntington.	182 *Polk.	206 Van Mons de Leon Leclerc.
160 Laure de Glymes.	183 *Pratt.	207 *Wadleigh.
161 *Lodge, *Bordenave*.	184 *Pulsifer.	208 *Washington.
162 Louise bonne of Jersey.	185 Quilletette.	209 *Weber's Autumnal.
165 Marie Louise.	186 *Rapelje.	210 *Westcott.
166 *McClelland.	187 *Raymond.	211 *Wilbur.
167 *Merriam.	188 *Rip Van Winkle.	213 *William (Edwards.)
168 Millot de Nancy.	189 Rodney.	214 *Williamson.
169 Napoleon.	190 *Selleck.	215 *Wollaston.
170 Niell.		

WINTER VARIETIES.

216 Alexandre Bivort.	239 Chaumontel, *only on quince.*	262 Mollett's Guernsey Beurré.
217 Alexandre Lambré.	241 Colmar, *only on quince.*	263 Monseigneur Affre.
220 Bergamot Esperin.	242 *Columbia.	266 Passe Colmar
221 Beurré Berckmans.	243 *Cross.	Pound, see 271.
222 Beurré Bretonneau.	244 Doyenné d'Alençon (*fine	267 *Prince's Perpetual, $1.
223 Beurré Bruneau.	winter.*)	268 *Reading.
225 Beurré d'Aremberg, (*un-*	245 Flemish Bon Chretien.	269 Soldat Laboureur.
thrifty, slow growth.)	246 Fondante de Noel.	270 St. Germain, Prince's.
226 Beurré Rance.	251 Fortunee.	271 St. Germain, Uvedale's,
227 Buerré Easter.	252 Glout Morceau,	*Pound.*
229 Beurré gris d'hiver nouveau	253 Grand Soleil.	272 Suzette de Bavay.
230 Beurré Langelier.	255 Jaminette.	273 Vicar of Winkfield.
232 Beurré, Winter (Rivers.)	256 Jean de Witt.	274 Vicompte de Spoelberch.
233 Bezi des Veterans.	257 Josephine de Malines.	275 Triomphe de Jodoigne.
234 Black Worcester (*baking.*)	259 *Lawrence.	276 Triomphe de la Pomologie.
235 *Bowne's Winter Russet.	260 *Lewis.	277 Winter Nelis.
237 Catillac (*baking.*)	261 McLaughlin.	278 Zephirin Gregoire.

The following Additional Varieties can be supplied, but not in as large quantities as the preceding.

281 Belle de Paris.	293 Colmar d'Alost.	305 Limon (Van Mons.)
282 Belle Julie.	294 Commodore.	306 Paternoster.
283 Beurré Bennert.	295 Comprette.	307 Prevost.
284 Beurré Citron.	286 Comte de Flandres.	308 *Rae's Bergamot or Egin.
285 Beurré d'Empereur Alex-	297 Delices de la Cour.	209 Rousselet Esperen.
andre.	298 Docteur Bouvier.	310 Rousselet de Meester.
286 Beurré Duhaume.	299 Groom's Princess.	311 Rousselet Enfant Prodigue.
287 Beurré Navez.	300 *Hamon.	312 *Styer.
288 Beurré Trigeur.	300½ Hovey (Dana's), $1 50.	313 *Taylor.
289 Bezi Sanspareil.	301 *Jackson.	314 Verulam.
290 Bezi tardif.	301 Henkel.	315 Vesouzière.
291 Camak's Georgian.	302 Henri Brevoort.	316 William Prince.
292 Charles Van Hoogten.	303 Inconnue Van Mons.	317 Zoar Beauty.
	304 Las Canas.	

N. B.—All the other finest European varieties, including the most new and rare, can be supplied 2 to 3 years budded on the Angers Quince.

REJECTED PEARS. The American Pomological Society have published a list of 451 *Rejected Varieties*, many of which are still offered for sale in Nursery Catalogues. Purchasers should look well to this important point.

Class I.—SUMMER PEARS.

Bartlett, large pyriform, clear yellow, often a blush, fine grained, very tender and buttery, sweet with a slight subacid, perfumed, moderately rich flavor, a splendid fruit, tree bears young, very productive, commands the highest market price.

Bean Present d'Artois, rather large, half melting, very juicy, fine flavor, first quality, tree vigorous and very productive. A new and highly esteemed variety.

Beurre Benoist, medium, melting, slightly perfumed, agreeable flavor, first quality, tree vigorous and productive.

Beurre Giffard, medium, melting, juicy, pleasant flavor, greatly esteemed, tree very productive, fruit larger than the Madeleine, and equally good.

Bloodgood, medium, obovate, yellow, russetty, buttery, sweet, rich aromatic flavor, rather slow growth, moderate crop.

Brandywine, medium, pyriform, yellowish green, melting, very juicy, fine flavor, tree very productive.

Canandaigua, has erroneously been called *Catharine,* very much resembles the Bartlett, but not quite as large or as good; tree vigorous and very productive, the fruit ripens at same period as the Bartlett.

Dearborn's Seedling, small, turbinate, clear yellow, fine grained, melting, juicy, fine flavor, but has been unduly extolled, when its size and quality are contrasted with others; tree of slow growth, bears young.

Doyenne d'été, small, obovate, yellow, bright, red cheek, melting, juicy, sweet, pleasant, not high flavor, tree bears very young.

European Honey, medium or under, roundish, yellow, sweet, good flavor, tree productive.

Heathcot, medium, obovate, pale whitish yellow, russetty, fine grained, very buttery, perfumed, excellent flavor, tree very hardy, and very productive.

Jargonelle, English, rather large, long pyriform, greenish yellow, brownish cheek, juicy, pleasant subacid, moderate flavor, very productive, valuable for market.

Kingsessing, rather large, obovate, green shaded, buttery, delicate, rich flavor.

Madeleine, medium, obovate, yellowish green, melting, very juicy, slight acid, delicate, agreeable refreshing flavor, vigorous growth, very productive; one of the best early Pears.

Moyamensing, rather large but variable, obovate pale yellow, buttery, melting, good flavor, productive.

Muscadine, medium, obovate, yellowish green, buttery, melting, somewhat coarse and astringent, rather rich, good flavor.

Osband's Summer, medium or under, obovate, yellow, reddish cheek, sweet, mild, and excellent flavor, one of the finest early Pears.

Queen of August, large, roundish ovate, very fair, pale yellow, tender, melting, buttery, juicy, pleasant flavor, excellent, tree very vigorous. A new and very valuable seedling variety, originated by ourselves, the largest of early pears, ripe during the last half of August.

Rostiezer, rather small, sometimes medium, pyriform, brownish green, reddish cheek, melting, juicy, sweet, very high perfumed flavor, of great excellence, one of the finest late summer pears.

Summer Francreal, medium, obovate, yellowish green, sometimes a blush, fine grained, buttery, melting, rich and excellent, much esteemed; tree thrifty, very productive.

Tyson, medium, pyriform, bright yellow, reddish cheek, fine texture, buttery, very melting and juicy, nearly sweet, perfumed, high and excellent flavor, tree vigorous, very productive.

Williams's Early, rather small, roundish, bright yellow, half buttery, juicy, somewhat musky, rich flavor, handsome.

Class II.—AUTUMN PEARS.

Henry IV., medium, obovate, greenish, yellow, melting, juicy, rich, perfumed, mostly first rate in flavor, tree vigorous, very productive.

Andrews, medium, pyriform, fair, yellowish green, reddish cheek, very juicy, melting, very agreeable flavor, very productive.

Beurre Bose, rather large, pyriform, deep yellow, buttery, juicy, sweet, perfumed, excellent; growth slow, fair crop.

Beurre, Brown, large, oblong obovate, yellowish green, russeted, very juicy, melting, buttery, rich subacid vinous flavor; much esteemed, growth slow and flexuose, and requires high cultivation.

Beurre d'Amanlis, large, obovate, yellowish green, some russet, reddish cheek, buttery, melting, juicy, rather rich, good, not high flavor. growth vigorous, productive.

Beurre d'Amanlis panaché, fruit similar in quality to the preceding, but both the wood and the fruit singularly striped with red and yellow,

Beurre d'Anjou, rather large, obovate, greenish yellow, somewhat russeted, red cheek, fine grained, buttery, melting, rich, vinous, delicious flavor.

Beurre Bachelier, large, fair. yellow, buttery, rich flavor, excellent, first rate, one of the most valuable new varieties.

Beurre Clairgeau, large, irregular pyriform, yellow, shaded with crimson and dotted over; flesh yellowish, buttery, juicy, sugary, perfumed, vinous flavor. A most splendid fruit, greatly esteemed; tree vigorous, early in bearing, very productive.

Beurre Diel, very large and splendid, obtuse pyriform, dull yellow, some russet, buttery, juicy, rich, firm flavor, vigorous growth, productive, and on the Quince often weighs a pound.

Beurre, Golden Bilboa, medium, obovate, fine yellow, some russet, fine grained, very buttery, melting, moderately rich, sometimes a slight acid astringency, not high flavor, productive.

Beurre Langelier, large and handsome, juicy, melting, high flavor, excellent, first quality, tree vigorous and productive.

Beurré Superfin, large, handsome, buttery, melting, high flavor, very excellent, one of the finest varieties, tree vigorous and productive.

Bergamotte Cadette, or Beurré Beauchamps, medium, roundish obovate, greenish yellow, often russeted, with reddish brown cheek, buttery, melting, sweet, quite rich, slightly perfumed, excellent, productive, highly esteemed.

Bergamotte, Gansels, medium, rather large, roundish, oblate, yellowish brown, faint brownish blush, melting, juicy, sweet perfume, rich, first rate flavor, highly esteemed.

Bergen, large, turbinate, yellow, red cheek, buttery, juicy, melting, sweet, excellent flavor.

Beurré Van Marum, medium, or rather large, pyriform, yellow, juicy, melting, sweet, very agreeable flavor, estimable, tree productive, and soon in bearing.

Bezi de Montigny, medium, obovate, yellowish green, half buttery, melting, juicy, sweet, persumed, good flavor.

Buffum, a seedling of the white Doyenné, medium, fair, obovate, yellow, reddish cheek, somewhat russeted, buttery, sweet, good flavor, tree very vigorous, produces great and regular crops.

De Louvain, distinct from Beurré de Louvain, which is a baking pear, medium, obovate, light yellow, somewhat russeted with reddish dots, buttery, melting, rich, fine flavor, an estimable variety.

Dix, large, pyriform, deep yellow, sweet, juicy, rich, excellent, sometimes rather acid, valuable, very tardy in bearing.

Doyenne Boussoch, large and showy, thick obovate, lemon yellow, somewhat russeted, often a reddish cheek, buttery, melting, very juicy, first rate flavor.

Doyenne, Gray, medium, obovate, cinnamon russet, very buttery, melting, rich, perfumed, delicious flavor, much esteemed, very productive.

Doyenne Sieulle, medium, roundish, obtuse, pale yellow, slight blush, fine grained, buttery, rich, excellent flavor, tree vigorous, productive.

Doyenne, White. This is the Virgalieu of the New York markets, and the Butter Pear of Philadelphia. Medium, or rather large, obovate, fine grained, buttery, melting, juicy, rich, excellent flavor, none more esteemed, commands the highest price; tree of vigorous growth, and produces great crops on standard trees in the interior of this State, and on the Quince it yields well everywhere. The Striped Doyenne is valueless.

Duchesse d'Angouleme, very large, often weighing a pound or more, obovate, greening yellow, rather coarse, buttery, juicy, very good on Quince, worthless on the pear stock.

Duchesse d'Orleans, medium to large, pyriform golden yellow, often russeted, red cheek, buttery, melting, rich, delicious, very handsome.

Dunmore, large, oblong obovate, greenish with brownish russet dots, buttery, melting, perfumed, rich, fine flavor, growth vigorous, productive.

Flemish Beauty, large and splendid, always fair, obovate, reddish brown russet on pale yellow ground, juicy, melting, usually very rich, sweet, and excellent flavor, but variable, and sometimes not highly flavored, a very valuable fruit, tree vigorous, productive.

Fondante d'Automne, or Belle Lucrative, medium, obovate, yellowish green, slightly russeted, fine grained, very juicy, melting, rich, perfumed, excellent, one of the finest of pears, tree vigorous, very productive, and comes soon into bearing.

Fondante de Malines, medium size, melting, very juicy, excellent flavor, first rate, one of the finest new varieties, tree hardy and vigorous, succeeds well on the Quince.

Frederick of Wurtemberg, large and beautiful, short pyriform, yellow, brilliant red cheek, very melting, buttery, juicy, variable in quality, sometimes delicious, often inferior, tree very vigorous, productive, a beautiful market fruit.

Fulton, nearly medium, roundish oblate, dark cinnamon russet, half buttery, melting, sprightly, agreeable rich flavor, estimable, tree vigorous, produces large and regular crops.

Jalonsie de Fontenay, medium, thick pyriform, yellowish green, somewhat russeted, often faint red cheek, buttery, melting, mild, rich, fine flavor, estimable.

Louise Bonne of Jersey, large, pyriform, yellowish green, dull red cheek, very juicy, buttery, rich, faintly subacid, fine flavor, tree vigorous, very productive, succeeds admirably on Quince, and is relied on for its great crops, and as a favorite market fruit.

Marie Louise, crooked and irregular growth, fruit large, pyriform, yellowish, somewhat russeted, buttery, melting, vinous, rich, five flavor, but variable, and often 2d or 3d rate. Requires high cultivation to perfect the fruit.

Napoleon, medium, pyriform, yellowish green, extremely juicy, melting, moderately rich, good flavor, sometimes astringent, tree hardy, thrifty, very productive.

Nouveau Poiteau, above medium, obovate, pale green, with a few blotches of russet, fine grained, melting, juicy, rich aroma, excellent, very highly esteemed, tree vigorous and bears promptly and abundantly.

Onondaga or Swan's Orange, very large and splendid, obtuse oval, rich yellow, often brown cheek, slightly coarse, buttery, melting, rich, high flavor, estimable but not first quality, vigorous growth, productive.

Oswego Beurré, medium, obovate, yellowish green, melting, juicy, fine sprightly vinous flavor at first, then becoming nearly sweet, tree very hardy and vigorous, and greatly productive, an estimable and reliable variety.

Paradise d'Automne, rather large, pyriform, deep yellow, same appearance and qualities as the Beurre Bose, more melting and sprightly, and the growth more vigorous, which gives it a decided preference.

St. Michael Archangel, large, pyriform, greenish yellow, russeted crown, rather coarse, half melting, juicy, rich, good but not high flavor, about equal to the Bartlett.

Seckel, a tree of slow, compact growth, fruit small, in clusters, yellowish brown, deep dull red cheek, fine grained, sweet, very juicy, melting, buttery, delightful musky aroma, the richest and highest flavored of pears. Requires a rich soil and high culture.

St. Ghislain, medium, pyriform, pale yellow, buttery, juicy, fine flavor, estimable, tree vigorous, productive.

Stevens' Genesee, large, round obovate, often flattened, half buttery, sweet, rich, fine flavor, nearly first rate, tree vigorous, productive.

Triomphe de Jodoigne, very large, pyriform, deep yellow, dark red cheek, juicy, melting, good flavor, growth vigorous, productive.

Urbaniste, rather large, obovate, pale yellow, slightly russeted, melting, buttery, delicious perfumed flavor, very fine, growth vigorous.

Van Assche (Van Assene, erroneously), rather large, obovate, dull yellow, buttery, melting, rich fine flavor.

Van Mons Leon le Clerc, very large and splendid, long pyriform, yellowish green, fine grained, buttery, melting rich, fine flavor, the body and branches are grooved, and have an unthrifty appearance, productive.

Washington, medium, obovate, clear yellow, red dots on sun side, very juicy, melting, rich, perfumed, very sweet, first rate flavor, tree vigorous, very productive.

CLASS III.—WINTER PEARS.

Alexandre Bivort, medium, greenish, russet, juicy, very melting, sweet, very highly perfumed, excellent flavor, succeeds well on quince.

Beurré d'Aremberg, large, short pyriform, greenish yellow, partially russeted, buttery, melting, rich subacid flavor, very productive, tree unthrifty, of slow growth, the shoots covered with small wart-like excrescences. It should be superseded by the Soldat Laboureur and Gloux Morceau.

Beurré Easter, large, obovate, yellowish green, partially russeted, reddish cheek, fine grained, very buttery, melting, and when well ripened of excellent first rate flavor, tree vigorous, and succeeds well on quince.

Beurré Rance, medium, pyriform, dark green, melting, sweet, juicy, fine flavor, better at the South than at North, tree vigorous, productive.

Beurré gris d'hiver nouveau, medium, obovate, greenish, considerably russeted, buttery, melting, very juicy, rich, slight subacid, resembling in flavor the Beurré d'Aremberg, very valuable.

Chaumontel, succeeds only on quince, a large, noble fruit, pyriform, yellowish mingled with brownish red, deep red cheek, buttery, melting sugary, excellent flavor, it requires warm rich culture.

Doyenne d'Alencon, or **Doyenne d'hiver nouveau** medium, obovate, yellowish green, buttery, melting, excellent flavor, highly esteemed, keeps well through the winter, tree vigorous, and exceedingly productive. This is a most valuable and reliable fruit to grow for the markets and for exportation. It succeeds well on both Quince and Pear.

Fondante de Noel, or **Belle de Noel**, medium, obovate, greenish yellow, dark red cheek, melting, juicy, fine flavor, much esteemed.

Giant Morceau, large, short pyriform, greenish yellow, fine grained, buttery, melting, sweet, without acid, rich, excellent flavor, tree exceedingly vigorous and productive, succeeds remarkably well on the Quince. This is the *original and true* Beurre d'Aremberg. The blunder of substituting an erroneous one originated at Boston, as we may explain hereafter.

Josephine de Malines, medium, roundish, obovate, yellow, blush cheek, melting, juicy, vinous, fine flavor, greatly esteemed, and by many placed in the highest rank.

Lawrence, rather large, melting, juicy, rich flavor, much esteemed, tree very hardy, very vigorous, and exceedingly productive. It is admirably suited for barreling to send to our distant cities, and for exportation, and is destined to be among Pears what the Newtown Pippin is among Apples.

Passe Colmar, medium, pale yellow, fine grained, buttery, juicy, sweet, rich, excellent, first rate flavor, tree of flexuose, irregular growth, over productive, and the fruit must be thinned out.

Prince's Perpetual, medium size, fair quality, portable when fully matured, excellent for cooking, will keep till June, produces great crops.

St. Germain, Prince's, rather large, obovate, green, much russeted, dull red cheek, melting, juicy, slightly vinous, very agreeable fine flavor, one of the very best winter pears, tree vigorous, very productive. This is a most valuable Pear to be grown for barreling and supplying our distant markets, or for exportation.

Soldat Laboureur, large, yellow, buttery, melting, high flavored, excellent, first rate, tree very vigorous and productive. This is much to be preferred to the Beurre d'Aremberg, which is similar in quality, but of very unthrifty growth, and advances but slowly in comparison with this variety.

Suzette de Bavay, yellow, speckled reddish brown, very juicy, half melting, sweet, high flavor, excellent, greatly esteemed.

Vicar of Winkfield, large, very fair and handsome, long pyriform, yellowish green, dull red cheek, buttery, juicy, good second rate flavor, sometimes slightly astringent, but when ripened in a warm temperature is a good dessert pear, tree very vigorous, exceedingly productive, forms a noble tree even on the Quince stock. The long keeping of the fruit renders it eminently valuable, and it may be grown most profitably for market and exportation to any extent.

Vicompte de Spoelberch, medium or rather large, obovate, yellow, purplish cheek, buttery, melting, rich, fine flavor, requires good soil and culture.

Winter Nelis, medium or under, roundish, obovate, yellowish green, much russeted, fine grained, buttery, very melting, rich, sweet, perfumed flavor, growth slender, flexuose and straggling, very productive, early in bearing.

CLASS IV.—BAKING AND STEWING PEARS.

Black Worcester (Iron Pear of Boston), rather large, short ovate, dark russet on light green surface, firm, coarse, rather austere, cooks well, rich flavor, highly esteemed, tree of straggling growth, produces heavy crops, very profitable for market.

Bonchretien, Flemish, medium, obovate, pale green, brown cheek, crisp, juicy, tender when cooked, a first rate culinary fruit throughout the winter.

Catillac, very large, turbinate, yellow, often reddish cheek, firm, but valuable for cooking, becomes tender and excellent.

Uvedale's St. Germain, or Pound, very large, has weighed two pounds, pyriform, yellowish green, brown cheek, solid, long keeping, a first rate culinary pear, tree vigorous, attains the loftiest dimensions, producing great and regular crops. Quantities are sold in New York for exportation, and it may be grown and barreled with as much facility as Apples are.

---·◆·---

CHERRIES—PRUNUS CERASUS.

Standard Trees of large growth, 2 to 3 years, . . . 37 to 50 cts.
Pyramid and Dwarf Trees, of low growth, 2 and 3 years, . . 37 to 50 cts.
Trees of both the above classes, 4 to 7 years old, in a bearing state, 75 cts. to $1, and $1 50
Dwarf Standards on Mahaleb, ... 37 to 50 cts.

Note.—All the Cherries we cultivate for the North and West, are on the hardy Mahaleb and Morello Stocks, as Trees on the Mazzard stock will scarcely survive the severe winters of those regions. The Duke, Kentish, and Morello Varieties are much more hardy than the Heart and Bigarreau Varieties.

HEART CHERRIES.

1 Adam's Crown.
2 American Amber
3 Belle d'Orleans.
4 Black Eagle.
5 Black Tartarian.
6 Brandywine.
6½ Champagne.
7 Coe's Transparent.
8 Columbia, *new*, $1.
9 Conestoga.

10 Cumberland. (? *syn.*)
11 Downer's Late.
12 Downton.
13 Early Purple Guigne.
14 Golden Guigne.
15 Hertfordshire Black (sweetest.)
16 Hovey.
17 Knight's Early Black.

18 Manning's Mottled.
19 Monstrueux de Jodoigne.
20 Prince's Early Black Heart.
21 Prince's Large Black Heart.
22 Sparhawk's Honey.
23 Turkine, or Turkish, 75 cts.
24 Wendell's Mottled.
25 Werder's Early Black.
26 White French Guigne.

BIGARREAU CHERRIES.

27 Bigarreau d'Esperen.
28 Bigarreau of Mezel.
29 Black Bigarreau of Savoy.
31 China Bigarreau.
32 Downing's Red Cheek.
33 Early Black Bigarreau.
34 Early Mazan, *rare*, 75 cts.
35 Elton—Flesh colored Bigarreau.
36 Florence.

37 Graffion—Bigarreau.
    Yellow Spanish.
    Holland, *proved Napoleon.*
38 Large Heart-shaped.
    Gros Cœuret.
    N. B. *Very different from No.*29.
39 Large Red Proof (*largest.*)
    Great Bigarreau. Downing.
40 Late Black Bigarreau.
41 Maubec, *rare*, 75 cts.

42 Napoleon.
    Holland Bigarreau?
43 Reverchon, 75 cts.
44 Toupie de Henrard, *splendid,* 75 cts.
    Large Bleeding Heart.
45 Tradescant, Black.
    Elkhorn.
46 White Bigarreau.
    White Ox Heart.

DUKE AND KENTISH CHERRIES.

47 Admirable Soissons, *fine late,* 75 cts.
48 Archduke.
49 Belle Magnifique.
    Magnifique de Sceaux.
    Belle de Chatenay.
50 Belle de Choisy.
51 Carnation.
52 De Planchoury.

53 De Spa, or Donna Maria.
54 Duchesse de Palluau.
55 Kentish—Early Richmond.
56 Imperatrice Eugenie, $1.
57 Jeffrey's Duke.
58 Late Duke—June Duke.
59 Latest Duke, *extra*, 75 cts.
60 May Duke.

61 Reine Hortense.
    Monstrueuse de Bavay.
    Lemercier—Louis 18.
    Seize à la livre.
62 Royal Duke, (*late, estimable.*)
63 Vail's August Duke.
64 Varennes, *fine late Kentish.*
65 White Pearl, *new,* 75 cts.

MORELLO CHERRIES.

66 English, *large, estimable.*
67 Imperial, *late.*

69 Natte precoce—Double
    Natte, *early.*

70 Plumstone, large, *very good.*

ORNAMENTAL.

71 Chinese Double Pink.
72 Dwarf Double Flowering
73 Large Double Flowering.
74 Perfumed Austrian.

75 Weeping, $1 to $2.
76 European Bird Cherry, beautiful.

77 American Bird Cherry, 25c.
78 Red Cornelian.
79 Yellow Cornelian.

OHIO VARIETIES.

50 Black Hawk.
81 Brant.
81½ Carmine Stripe.
82 Cleveland.
83 Delicate (Kirtland.)
84 Doctor.
85 Early Prolific.
86 Favorite (Elliott's.)
87 Governor Wood.

88 Hoadley.
89 Jocosot.
90 Kennicott.
91 Keokuk.
92 Kirtland's Mary.
93 Late White Bigarreau.
94 Leather Stocking.
95 Logan.
96 Kirtland's Mammoth.

97 Ohio Beauty.
98 Osceola.
99 Pontiac.
100 Powhattan.
101 Red Jacket.
102 Rockport.
103 Shannon — Kirtland's Morello.
104 Tecumseh.

REJECTED CHERRIES.

The American Pomological Society has also rejected many other varieties, as announced in their publications.

American Heart.
Arden's White Heart.
Baumann's May.
Belle Agathe.
Bigarreau d'Octobre.
Black Heart (old variety.)
Black Mazzard.
Bowyer's Early Heart.
Burr's Seedling.
Buttner's October Morello.
Buttner's Yellow.
Coe's late Carnation.

Corwin.
Davenport.
Early May, or Indulle.
Early White Heart.
Gridley.
Hildesheim Bigarreau.
Holland Bigarreau, *synonym.*
Hyde's Red Heart.
Lindley.
Louis Phillipe.
Madison Bigarreau.
Manning's Early Black.
Manning's Early White.

May Bigarreau.
Merveille de Septembre.
October Bigarreau.
Ox Heart.
Red Bigarreau.
River's Early Amber Heart.
Robert's Red Heart.
Rumsey's late Morello.
Sweet Montmorency.
Tardive de Mans.
Waterloo, *dubious variety.*
Wilkinson.

Class 1.—HEART CHERRIES.

American Amber, medium, obtuse heart shape; dark pink color, tender, sweet, rich, excellent, tree very vigorous and productive, an indispensable variety. Ignorant persons condemn it, not having seen it, and confuse it with other varieties.

Black Eagle, medium, roundish, nearly black, very sweet and rich, high flavor, excellent.

Black Tartarian, quite large, splendid, heart shaped, shining black, half tender, consistent, sweet, rather rich, fine flavor, tree vigorous, remarkably upright, very productive.

Belle d'Orleans, earliest of all, white, shaded with pale red, tender, juicy, delicious, growth very vigorous, productive, highly esteemed.

Brant, large, heart shape, reddish black, half tender, sweet, juicy, rich flavor.

Champagne, (Downing,) medium, roundish, heart shape, bright red shaded, juicy, sprightly, rich flavor.

Columbia, a large and estimable Seedling variety, originated at Newtown, Long Island.

Cumberland, large, obtuse heart shape, purplish crimson, rather firm, fine flavor, first quality.

Coe's Transparent, medium, nearly globular, pale amber, red cheek, very tender, sweet, melting, excellent, tree very vigorous, productive.

Delicate, (Kirtland,) medium, roundish, yellow and light red, mottled, sweet, tender, juicy, high flavor, excellent.

Doctor, medium, roundish, pale yellow and red, sweet, tender, juicy, delicious flavor.

Downer's late red, medium, round heart shape, bright red, mottled with amber, tender, sweet, delicious, not subject to rot by rainy weather.

Downton, large round heart shape, cream color, shaded with red, tender, rich, delicious flavor.

Early Purple Guigne, very early, ripe next after Belle d'Orleans, and at same time as Baumann's May, size medium, heart shaped, dark red, nearly black, tender, sweet, juicy, rich flavor, tree less vigorous than most others of this class.

Early Black Heart, (Prince's,) medium to large, heart shape, black, tender, juicy, excellent, very estimable, tree vigorous and productive.

Favorite, (Elliott's) medium, round, yellow, marbled, carmine cheek, sweet, juicy, delicate, requires high culture to perfect its size and flavor, otherwise is inferior.

Golden Guigne, medium, round, bright golden color, honeyed sweet, tender, delicious, thin skin. beautiful, a very distinct fruit, tree vigorous, very productive, in clusters.

Governor Wood, largest size, roundish, pale yellow, marbled with carmine, half tender, sweet, juicy, rich, high flavor, very estimable.

Hovey, large, heart shape, amber nearly covered with bright red, rather firm, tender, sweet, fine flavor, tree vigorous, productive.

Jocosot, large, heart shape, shining liver color, almost black, tender, sweet, juicy, rich flavor.

Kirtland's Mary, large, roundish, light and dark, glossy red mottled on yellow, firm, sweet, juicy, rich, very high flavored.

Knight's Early Black, large heart shape, black, tender, juicy, very rich, high flavor, excellent.

Large Black Heart, (Prince's) considerably larger than the common Black Heart, (which we reject,) beautiful, shining black, obtuse heart shape, tender, sweet, juicy, excellent, first quality, tree exceedingly vigorous and productive.

Logan, medium, heart shape, purplish black, rather firm, sweet, juicy, rich flavor, tree hardy, vigorous, moderately productive.

Mammoth, (Kirtland's) very large, but not equal in size to the Large Red Prool, marbled with red, tender, sweet, juicy, fine flavor, and moderately productive.

Manning's Mottled, medium, round heart shape, amber mottled with red, tender, sweet, good flavor, second rate, productive.

Ohio Beauty, large, heart shaped, dark and pale red marbled, tender, juicy, high flavor, tree very vigorous, productive.

Osceola, medium to large, heart shape, purplish red, nearly black, sweet, juicy, rich flavor.

Pontiac, large, heart shape, purplish red, nearly black, tender, sweet, juicy, pleasant flavor.

Powhattan, medium, roundish, bright liver colored, half tender, sweet, juicy, pleasant, not high flavor, tree vigorous, productive.

Sparhawk's Honey, medium, round heart, pale amber to bright red, sweet, juicy, fine flavor, rather late, very productive.

Tecumseh, medium to large, heart shape, reddish purple, mottled, half tender, sweet, very juicy, not high flavor, hardy, late in blossoming.

Werder's Early Black, medium, roundish heart, purplish red, nearly black, tender, sweet, juicy, rich flavor.

White French Guigne, rather large, creamy white, sweet, tender, juicy, excellent, tree vigorous, very productive. White cherries are not so liable to attack from Birds, as Red and Black ones are.

Class 2.—BIGARREAU CHERRIES.

Bigarreau of Mezel, very large, heart shaped, dark red, firm, sweet, excellent, beautiful, highly esteemed, growth very crooked and irregular.

Black Bigarreau of Savoy, very large, roundish heart, shining black, beautiful, firm, fine flavor, excellent, tree vigorous, productive. One of the most admired and rare varieties.

Black Hawk, large, heart shape, deep purplish black, sweet, juicy, rich, fine flavor, estimable.

Buttner's Yellow, medium, roundish, pale yellow, firm, sweet, good flavor, late, tree vigorous.

China Bigarreau, medium, heart shape, amber, beautifully mottled with red, half tender, sweet, peculiar flavor, second rate, rather late. Grown from seed by William Prince.

Cleveland, large, roundish, bright red on yellow, juicy, rich, fine flavor, very vigorous, and very productive.

Elton, or Flesh-colored Bigarreau, large, pointed heart, pale yellow shaded red, flesh firm, becomes rather tender, rich, high flavored, excellent, one of the finest cherries in all respects.

Florence, large, heart shaped, amber, yellow marbled with red, red cheek, firm, sweet, juicy, rather late. Resembles Graffion, but later.

Graffion.—Bigarreau.—Yellow Spanish. This is not a genuine Bigarreau, that title applying only to *firm and crackling* cherries. Fruit very large, obtuse heart shaped, clear yellow, pale red cheek, beautiful, tender, rich flavor, excellent, tree vigorous, very productive. This variety is greatly esteemed for its size, beauty, and abundant crops. It was introduced by William Prince, from England, under the name of Yellow Spanish.

Keokuk, large, heart shape, dark purplish black, tender, rather coarse, deficient in flavor, does well for market, tree very vigorous.

Late White Bigarreau (Kirtland's), large obtuse heart shape, pale straw, bright red cheek, firm, sweet, juicy, pleasant flavor.

Leather Stocking, medium, heart shape, deep red at maturity, very firm, sweet, good flavor, bears distant transportation, vigorous, moderately productive.

Large Heart Shaped, or Gros Cœuret, very large, heart shape, shining blackish red, firm, sweet, rich, excellent flavor, a splendid fruit, tree vigorous, productive.

Large Red Prool, Great Bigarrean of Downing, introduced by William Prince from the south of France, the largest of all Cherries, oval, heart shape, splendid, shining blackish red, flesh red, firm, very sweet, rich, excellent flavor, tree very vigorous, productive; the first of Cherries in estimation. We have disseminated this splendid Cherry for above 30 years, and other Nurseries are now beginning to cultivate it.

Napoleon, very large, heart shaped, pale yellow spotted with deep red, very firm, fine flavor, scarcely first rate, rather late, tree vigorous, very productive, a suitable market fruit.

Red Jacket, large, heart shape, amber shaded with pale red, tender, juicy, good, but not of high flavor, very productive, ripens late.

Rockport, large, roundish, bright red mottled on pale yellow, firm, sweet, juicy, rich, delicious flavor, very vigorous, productive.

Touplé de Henrard, a large and remarkable cherry, oval with a point, sweet, rich, excellent.

Tradescant's Black, or Elkhorn, large, oval heart, black; flesh deep red, firm, leathery, not juicy, fine flavor, a very beautiful variety, ripening rather late after other kinds are scarce, well suited for distant carriage to market.

Wendell's Mottled, medium or large, obtuse heart, dark red nearly black, mottled, firm, crisp, high flavored, rather late.

Class 3.—DUKE, KENTISH, AND MORELLO CHERRIES.

The fruit of this class is generally round, or nearly so.

Belle de Cholsy, medium, pale amber, mottled with red, bright red cheek, very tender and very juicy, mild, subacid, nearly sweet, excellent, moderately productive.

Belle Magnifique, or Magnifique de Sceaux, quite large, rich, red, mild flavor, not highest quality, productive, one of the best late varieties.

Carnation, creamy white, mottled with red, firmer than others of this class, partially bitter at first, then mild acid, rich, pleasant flavor, second quality, distinct Spanish variety.

De Planchoury, large, dark red, sweet, tender, juicy, estimable.

Donna Maria, medium, dark red, tender, subacid, juicy, estimable for cooking, forms a small compact tree, very productive.

Duchesse de Palluau, large, dark red, acid, tender, juicy, excellent.

Jeffrey's Duke, medium, bright red, tender, juicy, rich, fine flavor, growth slow, very compact.

Kentish, or Early Richmond, medium, full red, acid, very juicy, fine flavor, excellent for early cooking, ripens early, and hangs long free from rot.

Late Duke, large, rich, deep red, subacid, not so rich as Mayduke, ripens very late, productive.

May Duke, or Holman's Duke. Three-fourths of the trees sold under this name are spurious, they being a late variety. The genuine is one of the earliest Cherries, large, red, becoming nearly black at full maturity, acid, very juicy, rich, excellent and grateful flavor, very hardy and productive.

Morello, English, medium to large, dark blackish red, rich, acid, slight astringency, juicy and good, very productive, growth slow, like all others of the Morello family.

Morello, Imperial, late, round, dark purplish red, tender, juicy, rich acid, estimable, very productive.

Morello, Plumstone, large, roundish heart, deep red, rich acid flavor, juicy, excellent, very late, the stone long and pointed.

Natte Precoce Morello, large, round, black, rich acid, earliest of its class.

Reine Hortense, large, sprightly subacid, juicy, rich, excellent, ripens late and hangs long, moderately productive, a valuable acquisition.

Royal Duke, very large, dark red, tender, juicy, rich, excellent, rather late.

Shannon, or Kirtland's Morello, medium, globular, deep purplish red, tender, juicy, acid, ripens late.

PLUMS—PRUNUS DOMESTICA.

Usual size, 50 cents each. Extra large trees, of bearing size, 4 to 7 years, $1 to $1 50.
Dwarf trees, 37 to 50 cents, according to age.
N. B. Above 30 varieties are never subject to knots in this part of the State.

1 Angelina Burdett.
2 Apricot (of Tours),
3 Bingham.
4 Bradshaw.
   Large Black Imperial.
5 Brevoort's Purple.
6 Buel's Favorite.
7 Campbell's Seedling.
8 Catharine, Schenectady.
9 Cherry, or Early Scarlet.
10 Cherry, Golden.
11 Chicasaw, Red.
12 Chicasaw, Late Red.
13 Chicasaw, Yellow.
14 Coe's Golden Drop.
15 Coes' Late Red.
   Red St. Martin.
16 Columbia, *very large.*
17 Cooper's Large Red.
18 Corse's Nota Bene.
19 Cruger's Scarlet.
20 Damson, September.
21 Damson, Shrophire.
22 Damson, Winter, or Late.
23 Date of Agen.

24 Denniston's Superb.
25 Denniston's Red.
26 Diaprée rouge.
   Mimms.
27 Double flowering, Large.
28 Double flowering, Dwarf or
   Sloe.
   The two last are Ornamental only.
29 Drap d'Or.
30 Duane's Purple French.
31 Early Favorite, Rivers.
32 Emerald Drop.
33 Fulton
33½ Gage, American Yellow.
34 Gage, Autumn.
35 Gage, Bleecker's.
36 Gage, English Yellow.
37 Gage, Dana's Yellow.
39 Gage, Green.
40 Gage, Hudson.
41 Gage, Imperial (Prince's.)
42 Gage, Red (Prince's.)
43 Gage, Prince's Yellow.
44 Gage, Purple.
45 Gage, Royal Green.

46 Gage, Schuyler.
47 Galbraith.
48 General Hand, *largest of all.*
49 Guthrie's Apricot.
50 Guthrie's Aunt Anne.
51 Guthrie's Topaz.
52 Hawkes.
53 Huling's Superb.
54 Imperatrice, Blue.
55 Imperatrice, Downton.
56 Imperatrice, Ickworth.
57 Imperial Milan.
58 Imperial Ottoman.
59 Imperial Purple.
60 Isabella.
61 Italian Damask.
62 Jaune hative.
   White Primordian.
63 Jefferson.
64 Jerusalem.
65 Late Black Orleans.
66 Large Red Toulouse
67 La Royale.
68 Lawrence's Favorite.

69 Lombard.	86 Orleans, Early.	101 Quetche, St. Martin's.
70 Long Scarlet—*Scarlet Gage.*	87 Orleans, Smith's.	102 Red St. Martin.
71 Madison.	88 Parsonage.	*Coe's late red.*
72 Magnum bonum, White.	89 Peach Plum.	103 Reagles Ancient City.
White Egg.	90 Perdrigon violet hatif.	104 Reagles Gage.
73 Magnum bonum, Yellow.	91 Prince Englebert.	105 Reagles Union Purple.
Yellow Egg.	92 Prince of Wales.	106 Reine Claude de Bavay.
74 Mamelounée.	93 Pond's Seedling (*English.*)	107 Reine Claude Diaphane.
75 Manning's Prune.	94 Precoce de Berthold.	108 Reine Claude d'Octobre.
76 McLaughlin.	95 Prune, Austrian.	109 Royale de Tours.
77 Masterion.	96 Prune, d'Agen, ⎫	110 Royale hative—*Early Royal.*
78 Martin's Seedling.	97 Prune, German, ⎬ *for*	111 St. Catherine.
79 Mediterranean.	*Guetche.* ⎭ *drying.*	112 Sharpe's Emperor.
80 Miller's Spanish, *very large.*	98 Prune, Italian, ⎰	*Dennyer's Victoria?*
81 Mirabelle tardive.	*Quetche d'Italie.*	113 Surpasse Orleans.
82 Monroe.	*Fellemberg.*	114 Thomas.
83 Mulberry.	99 Purple Favorite.	115 Washington.
84 Orange, *very large.*	100 Quackenboss.	116 Winter Bolmer.
85 Orange Egg, *very large.*		

Plum Trees of the following varieties are not subject to knots in the vicinity of New York, and are probably less so in any locality than any others:—

Nos. 4, 5, 9, 10, 11, 12, 13, 14, 15, 30, 35, 36, 41, 43, 49, 53, 54, 58, 61, 63, 72, 73, 84, 85, 89, 98, 102, 115.

REJECTED PLUMS.

The Pomological Society have published a list of 31 rejected varieties, which should receive the special attention of purchasers.

DESCRIPTIONS OF PLUMS.

Autumn Gage, medium, ovate, pale yellow, juicy, sweet, pleasant, free.

Bingham, large, deep yellow, red spots next sun, juicy, rich, delicious, handsome, productive.

Bleecker's Gage, medium, ovate, yellow, sweet, rich, luscious, free.

Bradshaw, very large and showy, oval, dark purple, juicy, good flavor, tree vigorous, erect, highly productive.

Campbell's Seedling, large, greenish yellow, very productive, late, valuable for market.

Cherry, or Early Scarlet, nearly medium, round, brilliant red, subacid, juicy, not rich, second rate, cling, tree vigorous, very ornamental by its early and profuse bloom. The Golden Cherry is similar in quality. Both are free from knots on Long Island.

Coe's Golden Drop, very large, oval, pale yellow, often dotted, firm, sweet, rich, not fine grained, cling, an excellent late variety.

Coe's Late Red, or Red St. Martin, medium, roundish, light purplish red, blue bloom, firm, rich, vinous; tree vigorous, very productive, a valuable very late variety.

Columbia, very large, handsome, globular, brownish purple, blue bloom, moderately juicy, rich, good flavor, rather coarse, not first rate, free, the fruit is liable to rot, tree very productive.

Denniston's Red, medium, ovate, pale red, fawn dots, rich, good second rate flavor, free.

Denniston's Superb, medium, roundish, yellowish green, mottled with purple, not juicy, but rich, vinous, and free.

Downton Imperatrice, unusually free from the curculio, medium, oval, pale yellow, acid becoming rather sweet, melting, valuable for preserves, ripens late.

Duane's Purple, very large, oblong oval, reddish purple, lilac bloom, moderately sweet, juicy, second rate flavor, cling, esteemed for its large size and beauty, a very profitable market fruit.

Emerald Drop, medium, long oval, yellowish green, juicy, rather rich, cling, second rate.

Fulton, medium, round, yellow, speckled, juicy, luscious, high flavor, late.

Galbraith, very estimable, early, large, oval, purple, tender, juicy, luscious, a cling.

General Hand, largest of plums, golden yellow, sweet, only moderate flavor, rather coarse, highly attractive for its size and beauty, tree remarkably vigorous, very productive.

Green Gage, the true variety is full medium, and not small as misrepresented, round, yellowish green dotted red at base, sweet, melting, aromatic, exceedingly rich. The tree is of so slow and unthrifty growth that it has been nearly abandoned; and the Imperial Gage, a seedling from it, now takes its place almost universally.

Guthrie's Apricot, large, roundish ovate, yellow, some crimson dots, juicy, sweet, moderate flavor, cling, very productive.

Highlander, large, ovate, deep blue, dotted, juicy, sugary, rich, vinous, excellent, end of September.

Huling's Superb, one of the largest, roundish, yellowish green, rather firm, sweet rich, sprightly, excellent, free, tree vigorous, large foliage.

Ickworth Imperatrice, medium or rather large, obovate, purple, sweet, juicy, rich flavor, ripens late, becomes drier and sweeter, and keeps into winter.

Italian Damask, medium, roundish, brownish violet, firm, sweet, high flavored, estimable, free, tree vigorous, productive.

Italian Prune, or Fellemberg, a most vigorous and productive tree, and unusually free from the

2

curculio and from knots. Fruit large, oblong, purple, handsome, estimable for dessert, and also for preserving, or drying.

Imperial Gage, large, oval, pale yellowish green, juicy, melting, rich, free, tree very vigorous, remarkably and regularly productive, better suited to all localities than any other variety. Always free from knots on Long Island. This and Italian Prune, and Guthrie's Apricot, hold their fruit better against the curculio than any others.

Imperial Milau, large, oval, deep purple, sweet, juicy, estimable.

Imperial Ottoman, medium, oval, greenish yellow marbled, sweet, very juicy, excellent, scarcely adhering, tree hardy, succeeds in Maine, exceedingly productive.

Jefferson, large, oval, greenish yellow, very juicy, rich, excellent, nearly free, one of the largest and most estimable.

Lawrence's Favorite, large, roundish, yellowish green, juicy, rich, excellent, high flavor, free.

Lombard, unusually free from the curculio, medium, ovate, violet red, pleasant flavor, not rich, but of fine quality, tree hardy, very prolific.

Long Scarlet, or Scarlet Gage, medium, oblong, yellowish red, bright red cheek, acid, juicy, rich, cling, good market fruit for preserves.

Magnum Bonum, Yellow, or Yellow Egg, very large, egg shaped, beautiful, coarse, but excellent for cooking, tree vigorous, very productive, profitable for market. The White variety differs only in being of a paler color, and the Red or Purple is so coarse it has been rejected.

Mammelonne, medium, round, greenish, red spotted, juicy, rich flavor, free.

Manning's Prune, or Long Blue, a good variety of German Prune, large, long oval, dark purple, blue bloom, firm, rather juicy, sweet, pleasant, free, very productive.

Marten's Seedling, large, deep yellow, blotched red, juicy, rich, sprightly, excellent, last of August.

McLaughlin, medium, roundish, russet yellow, tinged over with red, rather firm, sweet, juicy, excellent.

Orange, one of the largest, oval, yellow, showy, rather coarse, tree very vigorous and highly productive, a profitable market fruit, it is free from knots on this Island.

Orleans, Early, medium, ovate, reddish purple, second rate, moderate flavor.

Orleans, Smiths, large, ovate, dark reddish purple, blue bloom, juicy, rich, nearly first rate, tree very vigorous, productive in nearly all soils, shoots reddish purple, perfectly straight.

Peach, very large, roundish, varies from salmon to brownish red, juicy, sprightly, good flavor, free, rather coarse, but esteemed for its size, beauty, and early ripening, tree vigorous, productive.

Prince Englebert, oval, large, deep purple with bloom, juicy, rich, excellent flavor, freestone.

Prune d'Agen, a famous variety for drying as prunes, medium, oblong, purple, blue bloom, sweet, estimable, free, very late, profusely productive.

Purple Favorite, medium, or rather large, roundish, brownish purple, tender, juicy, sweet, excellent, free, tree grows slow.

Quackenboss, very large, fair, deep purple, juicy, exceedingly productive, very valuable for market, last of September.

Reagle's Ancient City, very large, deep yellow, carmine cheek, juicy, sugary, excellent, middle of August.

Reagle's Gage, medium, pale green, juicy, rich, luscious, late in August.

Reagle's Union Purple, large, deep purple, late, very valuable for market.

Reine Claude de Bavay, ovate, greenish yellow spotted red, rather firm, juicy, sugary, rich, excellent quality, adhering slightly, growth vigorous, very productive.

Red Gage, Prince's, medium, round ovate, brownish red, juicy, mild sweet, rich, unusually pleasant and refreshing flavor, free, tree vigorous, dark red shoots, very productive.

Royale Hative, or Early Royal, medium, roundish, pale purple, dotted, blue bloom, rich, high flavor, equal to the best Gages, freestone, last of July.

Schenectady Catherine, small, roundish, deep purple, violet, sweet, melting, rich, excellent, growth rather slender.

Shropshire Damson, small, same size as Winter Damson, obovate, purple, first quality for preserves, cling, tree much more vigorous than the White Damson, not so subject to knots, exceedingly productive. The Winter or Late Damson resembles this, but is very subject to knots.

Washington, very large, ovate, yellowish green with a blush, rather firm, sweet, mild, moderately rich, free, tree free of knots at Long Island.

Yellow Gage, Prince's, medium, oval, golden yellow, rich, sugary, melting, excellent, tree very vigorous and productive, and on Long Island is free from knots.

PEACHES—AMYGDALUS PERSICA.

Price, 25 cts., except where otherwise noted.

N. B.—Large quantities at very reduced prices. Trees suitable for Dwarfs or Espaliers can be supplied at 37 to 50 cts. Peaches on the Plum stock are valueless for Orchards.

FREE STONES, OR MELTERS.

1 Admirable, Early.	2 Admirable, Late.	
Belle de Vitry—Bon-Jard.	*Titon de Venus.*	4 Baltimore Beauty.
Belle de Paris.	3 Abricotée, 50 cts.	5 Barney.
	Yellow Admirable.	

6 Barrington.
7 Belle Bausse, *larger than No. 41.*
8 Bellegarde—Galande.
9 Bergen's Yellow.
10 Bourdine—Royale, *distinct from No. 2.*
11 Brevoort (Morris).
11½ Carpenter's White.
12 Chevreuse hative.
13 Chevreuse tardive.
    Bon Ouvrier.
14 Cole's Early Red.
15 Columbia, or Pace.
16 Cooledge's Favorite.
17 Cooper's Catherine.
18 Crawford's Early (Melacoton)
19 Crawford's Late (Melacoton).
20 Cutter's Yellow.
21 Delaware White.
22 Diana Freestone.
23 Double Montagne.
24 Druid Hill.
25 Dulaney's Heath, 50 cts.
26 Early Barnard (*Alberge*).
27 Early Chelmsford.
28 Early Newington (*Downing*).
29 Early Purple.
    Pourprée hative.
30 Early Sweetwater, *Prince.*
31 Early White Globe.
32 Early York, Large—George IV.
Haines' Early red—Honest John.
    Walter's Early?
33 Early York, Serrate.
34 Early Tillotson, *Mildews.*
35 Eliza Schmitz.
36 Fay's Early.

37 Fox's Seedling.
38 George IV., see Early York.
39 Gorgas, 50 cts.
40 Green Catherine.
41 Grosse Mignone (*true*).
43 Harker's Seedling.
44 Hative de Ferrieres, 50 cts.
45 Heath Freestone.
    Cole's White Melacoton.
46 Henry Clay.
47 Hill's Madeira.
48 Howard's Pound.
49 Hussman's Favorite.
50 June, *yellow flesh,* 50 cts.
50½ Late Delaware.
51 La Fayette.
52 La Grange, *snowwhite.*
53 Late White Free.
54 Madeleine de Courson.
    Red Magdalen.
55 Magdalen, White.
56 Malta.
57 Miller's Early Anne.
58 Morrissania Pound.
59 Nivette—Orange Free.
60 Noblesse.
61 Noblesse Seedling.
62 Nutmeg, Blush.
63 Nutmeg, White.
64 Oldmixon Free.
65 Orange Melacoton, *extra,* 50 cts.
66 Owen, 50 cts.
67 Perry's Seedling.
68 Petite Mignone.
69 Petit's Imperial.
70 Poole's Large Yellow.
71 President.
72 Prince's Paragon (true).

73 Prince's Excelsior, $1,00
74 Pucelle de Malines.
75 Rareripe, Beers' Late Red.
76 Rareripe, Borden's Late.
77 Rareripe, Golden.
78 Rareripe, Hastings.
79 Rareripe, Prince's Red.
80 Rareripe, Red (Morris).
81 Rareripe, White (**Morris**).
82 Rareripe, Yellow.
83 Rebold's Late Red.
84 Red Cheek Melacoton.
85 Reine des Vergers.
86 Reeves' Favorite.
87 Rose Hill Melacoton.
88 Royal Charlotte.
89 Scott's Early Red.
90 Scott's Nonpareil.
91 Scott's Magnate (Rareripe), 50 cts.
92 Scott's Nectar (Rareripe), 50 cts.
93 Scott's New White.
94 Smock Free.
95 Snow—*White Flowers.*
96 Strawberry, or Rose.
97 Stump the World.
98 Susquehanna.
99 Troth's Early Red.
100 Van Zandt's Superb.
101 Walburton Admirable, 50 cts.
102 Ward's Late Free.
103 Washington Rareripe.
104 Waxen Mignone.
105 Well's Free.
106 White Ball (Hovey).
107 White Imperial.

CLINGSTONES, OR PAVIES.

108 Admirable.
109 Blood (preserves).
110 Heath—Late Heath.
111 Howard's Splendid, 50 cts.
112 Howard's Superb, 50 cts.
113 Incomparable.
    Admirable rouge tardive.
114 Large White.
115 Lemon.

115½ Lyon.
116 Oldmixon.
117 Old Newington.
118 Orange, *Prince.*
119 Pavie de Pompone, *extra,* 50 cts.
    Monstrous Pompone.
120 Pavic tardive, *Poiteau,* 50c.
    October Scarlet.

121 Prince's Climax, 50 cts.
122 Prince's Fortunatus, 50 cts.
123 Rodman's Red.
124 Smith's Newington—Early Red.
125 Tippecanoe (Lemon).
126 Washington Cling.

NEW AND RARE PEACHES,
38 to 50 cents.
Those marked thus * are French and Italian; the others are mostly superior Southern varieties.

FREESTONES.

127 Amelia.
127½* Auger's Large Purple.
128 Baldwin's Late.
129 Baugh.
130 Camak's Serrate.
131 Canary.
131½ Carpenter's Carnation.
133* Chancelière à gros fruit.
134 Columbus June.
135* D'Asée très grosse, 75 cts.
136* De Colmar.
137* Déese hative.
138* Déese tardive.

139* De Quesnoy.
139½* De l'au, or D'Italie.
140 Edward's Late White.
141* Egyptienne, 75 cts.
142 Exquisite.
142½ Gregory's Late.
143* Grosse Mignone hative.
144 Golden Ball.
145 Honey (Chinese seed) $1,00
146 Hopkinsville.
147* Incomparable en beauté.
147½ Jane, *white flesh.*
148 Jones' Large Early.

149 Kentucky Favorite.
149½* Leopold I.
150 Lady Parham.
151 Large Crimson.
152* Madeleine rouge hative.
152½ Magee.
153* Mignonne frisé.
154* Mignonne tardive.
155* Monstrueuse de Doué.
156 Montgomery's Late.
157 Moore's June.
158 Mrs. Poinsett.
158½ New Malta (Henry Gouin).

159 President Church.
160 Pride of Autumn.
161* Princesse Marie.

161½* Ray Mackers.
162 Regent.
163 Sieulle.

164 Tecumseh.
165 Tinley's Superb yellow.
166 Violet hatif (smooth skin).

CLINGSTONES.

167 Bennett's Mammoth.
168 Blanton.
169 Bordeaux.
170 Calloway.
171 Catharine.
172 Chinese.
173 Clark's October.
174 Cowan's Late.
175 Demming's September.
176 Donahoo.
177 Dr. Cherry's November.
178 Early Red Cling.
179 Eaton's Golden.
180 Eliza Thomas.
181 Elmira.

182 Flewellen
183 Horton's Delicious.
184 Hull's Athenian.
185 Indian Blood.
186 Jackson.
187 Late White English.
188 Mammoth Cling.
189 Monstrous Cling.
190 Nix's Late White.
191 October Orange, extra 75 cts.
192 O'Gwynne.
193* Parie Alberge, ou Jaune.
194* Pavie de Dolo.

195* Pavie tardif de Berne.
196 Perry.
197* Persique, or Grosse Perse-que.
Pavie de Palmiers.
198 Prince's Golden, extra, 75 cts.
199 Red Winter (November).
200* Sanguinolle la grosse.
201 Shanghae.
202 Silver Peach (white blossom).
203 Stephenson.
204 Vanderveer.
205 White Globe.

ORNAMENTAL VARIETIES, 50 CENTS.

206 Double Red, or Rose flowering.
207 Double Madeleine, rose color.

208 Double Mignone, red.
209 Double Ispahan, small red.
210 Dwarf Orleans, bears fruit, unique.

211 Chinese Double Crimson, 75 cts.
212 Chinese Double White, 75 cts.

PEACHES SUPERSEDED BY SUPERIOR VARIETIES.

FREESTONES.

Acton Scott.
Belle Chevreuse.
Bloodgood's late Green.
Chancellor.
Chilian.
Early Anne.
Emperor of Russia.
Flushing.

Jacques Rareripe.
Kenrick's Henth.
Late or Large Melting.
Red Nutmeg.
Robinson Crusoe.
Royal George (mildews).
Siebolt.
Sulhampstead.

Swalsh.
Tice, or Tice's Early (poor bearer)
Weeping, Reid's.
White blossom Incomparable.
Yellow Alberge.
Yellow Nutmeg.

CLINGSTONES.

Carey's Mammoth.
Catherine.

Congress.
La Fayette.

Late Yellow Alberge.

SELECT PEACHES, FOR MARKET, ETC.

Admirable, Early, rather large, roundish, pale straw, marbled, with bright red next the sun, sweet, melting, rich flavor, a firm fruit, keeps well, and bears carriage, very productive.

Abricotée, or Yellow Admirable, very large, round, beautiful, orange color, flesh same color, pleasant Apricot flavor. A rare and estimable variety, ripening late in October, well suited to the South, but cannot mature north of this locality.

Barnard, Early (Alberge erroneously), rather large, deep yellow, red cheek, juicy, melting, good second rate, productive, inferior to Bergen's Yellow.

Barrington, large, regular oval, beautiful, pale straw, marbled with light red, very tender, sweet, very juicy, rich, and luscious, very estimable.

Bergen's Yellow, very large, roundish, deep orange, broad crimson cheek, juicy, rich, luscious, excellent, greatly esteemed.

Brevoort, medium, round, white, bright red cheek, sweet, rich, high flavor.

Cole's Early Red, medium, roundish, mottled red, bright red cheek, juicy, rich, fine flavor, early, very productive, white, bright scarlet cheek, melting, juicy, rich, faint acidity.

Cooledge's Favorite, medium, roundish, white, bright scarlet cheek, very melting, juicy, rich, faint acid flavor, much esteemed.

Crawford's Early (Melacoton), very large, oval, showy, yellow, red cheek, very juicy, faint acid, rich, good but moderate flavor, productive. A favorite market variety.

Crawford's Late (Melacoton), very large, roundish, splendid appearance, yellow, broad, deep red cheek, rich, juicy, vinous, good, but moderate flavor, productive. A very showy and favorite market variety.

Early Newington, of Downing (not Smith's Early Newington, which is a cling), an old variety renamed, medium size, roundish, white, marbled with red, rich, red cheek, juicy, fine rich flavor, early and valuable.

Early York, Large, or George IV. (also called by many other names), large, roundish, whitish, with red dots, deep red cheek, very juicy, mild, rich flavor, excellent, greatly esteemed. Originated, by William Prince, from the Red Rareripe.

Early York, Serrate, medium, roundish, ovate, greenish white, dark red cheek, tender, juicy, rich, slight acidity, very productive, early.

Early White Globe, ripens immediately after the Nutmegs, medium size, round, white, sweet, good flavor, not very juicy, a favorite and peculiar variety, differing from all others that ripen at the same period.

Fox's Seedling, rather large, round, white, red cheek, sweet, juicy, estimable, ripens late.

Grosse Mignonne, a rare variety, although the name is in every catalogue, *large flowers,* fruit large, rounded, some rather ovate, pale yellow, mottled with red and yellow, deep velvety purplish red, and red about the stem, juicy, melting, sweet, very rich, vinous flavor, luscious, unsurpassed.

Heath Freestone (this is not at all similar to Kenrick's Heath, as many erroneously state), rather large, oval, greenish straw color, often slightly shaded with red near the stem, flesh white to the stone, juicy, tolerably sweet, subacid, not high flavored, sometimes bitterish, second rate for dessert, but makes admirable preserves.

Heath Cling, very large, oval, white, tinged red next sun, quite downy, very juicy, sweet, high, rich, excellent flavor, it must be ripened in the house in same manner as pears, and then surpasses all other peaches in flavor.

Howard's Splendid, large, oval, white, sometimes tinged with red next sun, ripens late, suited to the South.

Large White Cling, large, round, beautiful, white, light red cheek, very juicy, sweet, rich, high flavored, delicious. It is best when ripened for four or five days in the house, which is the only proper course with all Clingstones.

Late Admirable, large, roundish, pale green, pale red cheek marbled with darker red, juicy, delicate, excellent flavor.

La Grange, rather large, oval, white, seldom any tinge of red, juicy, rich, fine flavor, much esteemed, ripens late.

Lemon Cling, very large, splendid, oval, rich yellow, bright red cheek, high lemon flavor, rich, aromatic, excellent, makes admirable dumplings and preserves.

Nivette, or Orange Free, large, ovate, pale lemon color, sometimes a faint red cheek, juicy, melting, very sweet, luscious, rich flavor, has few or no superiors.

Noblesse, large, ovate, pale green, dull red cheek, very juicy, rich, high flavor, delicious.

Oldmixon Free, large, roundish, white marked red, dark red cheek, tender, rich, luscious, excellent, very productive, a favorite market fruit.

Oldmixon Cling, large roundish oval, yellowish white dotted red, deep red cheek, juicy, rich, high flavor, productive.

Orange Melacoton, very large, splendid, roundish, deep yellow, broad deep red cheek, juicy, sweet, luscious, devoid of the acidity that attaches usually to yellow-fleshed peaches, a most estimable new variety.

Pavie de Pompone, or Monstrous Pompone, the largest of peaches, ovate, greenish yellow marbled with red, very dark red cheek, juicy, sweet, rich, fine flavor, requires a long summer to mature in this latitude, well suited to the South. Distinguishable by its broad foliage and vigorous growth. Flowers small. Nearly all sold under this name are spurious, and even Mr. Downing never saw the genuine, and states mistakenly that it has large flowers.

Pavie Tardive, or October Scarlet, small flowers, large, ovate, beautiful, palestraw, deep red cheek, sweet, juicy, excellent, very productive. It is the most valuable of all late peaches to grow for the market, but is rarely to be met with in the nurseries.

President, rather large, ovate, white, dull red cheek, very juicy, luscious, fine flavor.

Prince's Climax, large, oval, yellow, crimson cheek; flesh yellow, very rich, pineapple flavor, middle Sept.

Prince's Excelsior, very large, round, splendid, entirely bright orange color, flesh golden yellow to the stone, parts freely, sweet, very juicy, extra rich, delicious, exquisite orange flavor, none superior, a remarkable acquisition, ripens middle of October, well suited to the South.

Prince's Fortunatus, a cling, medium size, yellow, red cheek, ovate, very productive; withstands the Yellows better than almost any other variety.

Prince's Paragon, large, showy, oval, pale yellow, slightly red shaded cheek, juicy, rich, luscious, fine flavor. An erroneous variety is often sold under this name.

Rareripe, Golden, large, yellow, red cheek, juicy, rich, good flavor, handsome.

Rareripe, Morris' Red, rather large, white, dark red cheek, juicy, rich, high flavored, excellent.

Rareripe, Prince's Red, later than the preceding, large down to medium, roundish, pale yellow, partially reddened next sun, sweet, juicy, rich, very luscious, first quality.

Rareripe, Morris' White, medium, roundish, white, sometimes purple tinge on cheek, juicy, melting, rich flavor, much esteemed.

Rareripe, Yellow (Yellow Alberge of some), large, roundish oval, deep orange, rich red cheek, mealy, without juice until fully ripe, then sweet, juicy, rich, good flavor, second rate,

Red Cheek Melacoton, large, ovate, yellow, deep red cheek, juicy, rich, luscious flavor, very productive, estimable for market.

Scott's Magnate (Rareripe), very large, splendid, roundish, oblate, whitish, deep red cheek, flesh white, juicy, excellent, a new and very beautiful variety.

Scott's Nectar (Rareripe), large, roundish, whitish, bright red cheek, flesh white, very sweet, delicious flavor, a beautiful and excellent new variety.

Scott's Nonpareil, large, roundish, deep yellow, red cheek, flesh yellow, sweet, juicy, and fine flavor, resembles Crawford's Late, but far superior in quality.

Snow, small white blossoms, fruit white, rather large, globose, melting, juicy, sweet, rich, sprightly.

Strawberry, or Rose, medium, oval, mostly marbled with deep red, melting, rich fine flavor, early.

Stump the World, large, ovate, white, red cheek, juicy, rich, fine flavor, productive, a favorite market fruit.

Tippecanoe, a Lemon Cling variety, very large, ovate, yellow, red cheek, flesh yellow, juicy, good vinous flavor, end of Sept.

Van Zaut's Superb, medium, oval, white beautifully mottled with red, sweet, juicy, fine flavor. A spurious round variety is almost universally disseminated by this name.

Washington Cling, medium, roundish, yellowish green, tinge of red on cheek; flesh very juicy, very sweet, luscious flavor, end of Sept.

NEW AND RARE PEACHES.

FREESTONES—*White Flesh.*

Baldwin's Late, large, oblong, white, red cheek, firm, melting, good flavor, October.

Bangh, medium, globose, straw white, with blush, melting, sweet, pleasant, Oct.

Columbus June, large, straw white, red cheek, melting, high flavor, excellent, July.

Edward's Late White, large, roundish, white, red cheek, sweet, juicy, excellent flavor, Oct.

Gorgas, rather large, roundish, straw white, shaded red cheek, saccharine, exceedingly luscious.

Native de Ferrieres, medium, roundish, white nearly covered with red, melting, sweet, rich, vinous flavor, end of August.

Honey, new, one of the most delicious.

Jane, very large, roundish, straw white, red cheek, melting, delicious, end of Sept.

Lady Parham, large, roundish, straw white, downy, firm, rich, vinous flavor, excellent, Oct.

Moore's June, under medium, globose, yellow marbled with red, juicy, vinous, very pleasant, July.

Montgomery's Late, large, round, straw white, red cheek, downy, very melting, excellent flavor, Sept.

President Church, large, roundish ovate, pale red, mottled dark red, very melting, delicious flavor, an important acquisition, Sept.

Pride of Autumn, large, oblong, white, red cheek, firm, melting, high flavor, end of Oct.

FREESTONES— *Yellow Flesh.*

Canary, medium, ovate, bright, yellow, very melting, very rich Apricot flavor, early in Aug.

Mrs. Poinsett, large, globose, straw white, brown and red cheek, melting, excellent flavor, August.

Owen, large, round, rich yellow, purplish red cheek, very melting, delicious saccharine subacid flavor, middle Sept.

Susquehanna, very large, globose, melting, sweet, rich vinous flavor, early Sept.

CLINGSTONES OR PAVIES.

Blanton, large, oblong, rich orange, slight red cheek, flesh yellow, firm, profuse, vinous juice, delicious, superior to Lemon Cling, August.

Bordeaux, large, oblong, pale yellow, red cheek; flesh yellow, melting, excellent vinous flavor, one of best, August.

Chinese, large, globose, creamy white, marbled red; flesh white, very melting, excellent vinous flavor, early Sept.

Donahoo, very large, roundish, creamy white, tinged red cheek; flesh white, exceedingly juicy, equally as rich and luscious as the Heath Cling and more tender, a great acquisition, end of Sept.

Elmira, large, oval, greenish yellow, downy; flesh white, sweet, good, end of August.

Flewellen, large, globose, straw white, overspread with red shades, purplish red cheek;

flesh pale straw, sweet, very melting, high flavored, very desirable, end August.

Horton's Delicious, large, roundish ovate, creamy white, faint blush cheek; flesh white, melting, delicious, same flavor as Heath Cling, Oct.

Hull's Athenian, very large, oblong, straw white, marbled red cheek; flesh white, rather firm, rich, high, vinous perfumed flavor, a great acquisition, Oct.

Jackson, large, oblong, dark yellow, deep red cheek; flesh orange, juicy, rich, sprightly, delicious, one of best, Sept.

Stephenson, large, roundish, very downy, creamy white, flesh-colored cheek; flesh white, very melting, delicious, vinous flavor, one of best, middle Oct.

— ◦◦◦ —

NECTARINES—BRUGNONS.

Price 38 cents except those *noted.*

C denotes Clingstones—all others are Freestones.

N. B. Trees of all the varieties suitable for Dwarfs or Espaliers, at 37 to 50 cts.

1 Baker.	3 Boston or Lewis.	5 Desprès, 50 cts.
2 Balgoue.	4 Cambridge.	6 Downton.

7 Due du Tellier.	13 Hunt's Tawny.	18 Red Roman, C.—*Brugnon*
8 Early Newington, C.	14 Jaune lisse—Late Yellow.	*Violet.*
9 Early York.	15 Large early Violet, 50 cents.	19 Stanwick.
10 Elruge.	*Violette grosse.*	20 Violette hative. — Early
11 Golden, Prince's C., 50 cts.	16 New White.	*Violet.—Large Scarlet.*
12 Hardwicke Seedling.	17 Pitmaston Orange.	21 Violette sucré, 50 cts.

Rejected Varieties.—Broomfield, Murrey, Newington, Peterborough.

SELECT NECTARINES.

Boston, large, bright yellow, red cheek, flesh yellow, sweet, very agreeable flavor.

Downton, large, melting, rich, excellent, tree very hardy.

Early Newington, very large, rich, excellent, much esteemed.

Elruge, medium, juicy, melting, rich, excellent, one of the best.

Hardwicke Seedling, medium, melting, rich, very good; tree very hardy.

Hunt's Tawny, flesh yellow, melting, rich, fine flavor, early.

Imperatrice, large, juicy, melting, excellent flavor.

Large Early Violet, very large, juicy, melting, excellent, a rare and superior French variety.

New White, large, melting, rich, luscious; tree very productive, one of the most hardy and reliable for crops.

Pitmaston Orange, large, yellow, bright red cheek, flesh golden yellow, juicy, melting, very good; tree hardy, very productive.

Prince's Golden, large, splendid, golden yellow marbled with bright red, juicy, fine flavor, well suited for the South, but matures here also.

Red Roman, large and beautiful, rich, very good when fully ripe.

Stanwick, large, melting, rich, excellent quality, one of the finest.

Violette hative—Early Violet, medium, juicy, rich, excellent, one of the best.

APRICOTS—PRUNUS ARMENIACA.

38 to 50 cents except those *noted.*

N. B. Trees of all varieties suitable for Dwarfs or Espaliers, 50 cts.
Extra large Standards, bearing age, $1 to $1 50.

1 Alberge de Tours.	10 Lafayette, *largest fruit,* $1.	19 Shipley—Blenheim.
2 Alsace, very large, 75 cts.	11 Large Early.	20 Schuyler.
2½ Beaujé.	12 Large Early Red.	21 St. Ambroise.
3 Black or Purple, very hardy.	13 Moorpark.	22 Tardif d'Orleans, Late, 75
4 Breda or Holland.	14 Musch.	cents.
5 Burlington.	15 Peach or De Nancy.	23 Turkey.
6 Early Golden (Dubois).	16 Roman.	24 Versailles, 75 cts.
7 Early Peach.	17 Royal.	25 Viard, 75 cts.
8 Hemskirke.	18 Sardinian, 75 cts.	26 White Imperial, 75 cts.
9 Kaisha or Syrian.		

Rejected Varieties.—Brussels, Orange or Persian, Red Masculine, White Masculine.

SELECT APRICOTS.

Alsace, orange red, very large, juicy, rich, excellent; tree vigorous and hardy.

Black or Purple, round, medium size, purple, juicy, pleasant; a native of Siberia, very hardy, ripe in August.

Breda, small, round, deep orange and red, fair second quality, very productive, one of the most hardy, early in August.

Early Golden, very similar in size and quality to the above, and probably a seedling from it, hardy and every productive; middle July.

Early Peach, large, yellow and red, rich, high flavored, August.

Kaisha, medium, citron yellow, sweet, juicy, rich flavor, excellent, flesh transparent, sweet kernel, early in August.

Lafayette, very large, equal to a medium size peach, oblong, orange and red, rich, high flavored, delicious, the most splendid of all. An American seedling, very vigorous and very hardy.

Large Early, large, oval, yellow and red, juicy, good flavored, very vigorous, very productive, one of the most reliable for crops, early in August.

Large Early Red, large, roundish, deep yellow, juicy, rich flavor; tree vigorous and hardy.

Moorpark, large, roundish, yellow, red cheek, sweet, juicy, rich, excellent; tree very productive, August.

Peach or De Nancy, very large, roundish, yellow, red cheek, juicy, rich flavor, one of the finest; tree very vigorous, very distinct from the Moorpark, August.

Red Masculine, earliest of all, medium size, roundish, yellow and red, good second quality, very productive; tree vigorous, early in July.

Roman, large, sweet, good, but rather dry, useful for tarts and preserves; tree vigorous, hardy, and very productive.

Royal, large, oval, orange, juicy, rich, excellent flavor; tree vigorous and hardy, end of July.

St. Ambroise, large, juicy, pleasant flavor, one of the finest early varieties.

Viard, large, juicy, rich, excellent; tree hardy, vigorous, productive.

ALMONDS.

Those marked thus (†) are 37 cents, and the others 50 cents.
N. B. Sweet Almonds, for Orchards, $25 per 100.

1 †Sweet hard shell, *most hardy.*
2 Ladies' thin shell (*for the South*).
3 Princess or Sultan—Paper shell, (*for the South*)
4 Pistachia (*for the South*).
5 Long hard shell—A gros fruit.
6 †Great fruited, *Macrocarpa, most hardy.*

ORNAMENTAL VARIETIES.

7 Large double blush Corsican.
8 Dwarf double red, 25 cts.
9 Chinese Dwarf double white, 75 cts.

QUINCES.

No. 1 is at maturity in Sept. and Oct., and the others in Oct. and Nov. Nos. 4 and 5 will keep
well till January.

	Price—Cts.		Price—Cts.
1 Orange or Apple, *very large, excellent for preserves, very productive*...	25	7 Mahon or Spanish, *large, estimable*..	50
2 Pear shaped..............................	30 to 35	8 Imperial, *very large, round, fine*.....	50
3 Portugal, *very large and fine*........	35	9 Rea's Seedling, *very large, splendid, most estimable*.....................	50 to 75
4 Winter Pear shaped..............	38	10 Egyptian, *large, estimable*..........	$1 00
5 Anger's Orange, *large*............25 to 38		11 Chinese Pink flowering, fine foliage,	
6 Constantinople, *very large, estimable.*	75	*very large oblong fruit*............38 to 75	

N. B. Extra large-sized Trees, 7 years old, in a bearing state, at $1 each, and smaller sizes by
the 100 or 1,000, at low rates.
Note. The *Japan Quince—Pyrus Japonica*, of different varieties, will be found under head
of Ornamental Shrubs; and Quince Stocks for ingrafting Pears, will be found under the appropriate head.

MULBERRIES.

	Cents.		Cents.
1 Black English or Chinese, *very acid. tree tender*.....................	50 to 75	7 Alpine, or Moretti, *black fruit*......	25
2 Red American, *excellent fruit*.......38 to 50		8 White Italian....................	25
3 Black Circassian, *sweet fruit, hardy.*.	50	9 Lhou Chinese, *hybrid, white fruit, large foliage, superior for silk, new.*.	75
4 Downing's Everbearing, *fine fruit*...75 to $1		10 Paper Mulberry. (See Ornamental	
5 Hick's Everbearing, *fine fruit*......	50	Trees).	
6 Multicaulis, *good sweet fruit*........	25		

N. B. Mulberries for Silk Culture, by the 1,000, at low rates.

WALNUTS, CHESTNUTS, AND FILBERTS.

	Price.		Price.
1 Madeira Nut, (English Walnut)....37 to 50		14 Chinquapin, or Dwarf Chestnut....	50
2 Madeira Nut, *extra large size*.......	$1 00	15 Prince's Hybrid Dwarf Chestnut, *large fruit*......................	$1 00
3 Madeira Nut, Prolific Dwarf........	$1 00	16 Red Filbert, *red skin*.............	25
3½ Double Madeira Nut, or Noyer de Jauge.......................	$1 00	17 White do., *white skin*.............	25
4 Peccannut..........................	50	18 Spanish do., or Large Cobnut......	25
5 Shell-bark Hickory, or Kiskytom...37 to 50		19 Barcelona, or Spanish Filbert.......	25
6 Black Walnut, round..............	38	20 Prolific do., or Cobnut.	35
7 Butternut, oblong................	38	21 Cosford do., *thin shell*..	38
8 American Chestnut............25 to 38		22 Frizzled do., or Cutleaved	38
9 Spanish or Lisbon Chestnut........	50	23 Cobourg do...........	38
10 French Chestnut, *very large, fine fruit* 38 to 50		24 Piedmont do...........	38
11 Maron de Lyon Chestnut, *very large fruit*........................50 to $1		25 Purple leaved do., *ornamental*.	50
12 Prolific Chestnut, or Maron........	50	26 Constantinople Filbert, *a large tree*..	50
13 Downton Chestnut................	50	27 American Hazlenut.............	15
		28 Cuckold do. (Rostrata).......	25

N. B.—Extra large Trees of the five preceding kinds, 7 to 13 feet, $1 to $2.

MEDLARS, PERSIMONS, PAPAW, SHEPHARDIA, NANDINA, and other PROMISCUOUS FRUITS.

	Price.			Price.
1 Dutch Medlar	50	11 Smooth Papaw, *Custard apple*		50 to $1
2 No tingham do., *small fruit*	50	12 Shepherdia argentea—Buffalo berry		50
3 Seedless do.	50	13 Nandina domestica (Chinese)		75
4 Monstrous fruited Medlar	50	14 Pistachia vera		75
5 Japan Medlar, or Loquat, *splendid evergreen foliage, fruit in clusters*	$1 50	15 Pistachia, Chinese		75
		16 Psidium Cattleyanum (Chinese Guava)		75
6 Diospyros kaki, Chinese Medlar	1 50	17 Aestomulus ferruginea (Japan)	$1	00
7 American Persimon	25	18 Zizyphus sativa—Jujube plum	1	00
8 American Persimon, *extra large trees*	$1 00	19 European Olive, 4 Fine Varieties		$1 to $2
9 European Date Plum, or Lotus	50	20 Bananas, Plantains, Dates, &c.		
10 Pierquin do	$1 00			

SELECT FIGS—FIGUIERS.

The culture of this delicious fruit has recently become an object of particular attention, and the Trees require no more care or protection in winter than the delicate kinds of Grapes, and can be grown at Baltimore, and South of it, in any quantities for market; and we may soon expect the markets of New York and other Northern cities to be supplied from the more Southern localities. The Trees are exceedingly productive and produce two regular crops in a season. We have rejected a number of varieties, such as Cypré, Clementine, &c., which have been found the least worthy of culture.

Those marked ‡, 50 cents. Those not marked are 75 cents. By the hundred, a discount of one third in price will be made; and where 25 or more are taken, 25 per cent. discount. When a dozen are taken of 6 varieties, 2 each, the price will be $1 50.

1 Adam's Fig, *enormous size*,$2.	13 ‡Golden, Large. — Jaune grosse.	28 ‡Napolitaine, or Naples, *twice bearing.*
1½ Allen's Large late White, *extra hardy.*	14 Grosse Longuette.	29 ‡Nerii, *exquisite.*
2 ‡Augelique, *white.*	15 Guignard, *estimable.*	30 ‡Oiel de perdrix.
3 ‡Black St. Michael, *delicious, great bearer, early.*	16 Habicon blanc.	31 Petarelle.
	17 ‡Habicon noir, *round.*	32 Pied de Bœuf.
4 ‡Bonne Dame, *early.*	18 Ischia, Black.	33 Poulette.
5 ‡Bourjasotte grise, or Early Yellow.	19 ‡Ischia, white or green, *excellent.*	34 ‡Pregussata, *excellent,white.*
6 ‡Brown Malta.	20 ‡Large Blue.	35 Red fruited Bordeaux.
6½ ‡Brown Ischia.	21 Large White, *ex. hardy.* 2 cr.	36 Rose Beyronue.
7 ‡Brunswick, *large, excellent.*	22 ‡Late Black St. Michael, *large, very productive, excellent, produces 3 crops.*	37 ‡Turkey, Brown, *gr. bearer.*
8 Camak's Large White, *fine, extra hardy.*		38 ‡Turkey, White.
		39 Twice bearing Grecian.
8½ Col. de Signora.	23 Longue Printaniere.	40 Vermissengue.
9 ‡Datte, on Quotidienne.	24 Madeleine, *very early.*	41 ‡Verte grosse.
10 Early White St. Michael, or Early May, *small,* 3 crops.	25 ‡Marseilles, *white, excellent. White Naples,* 2 crops.	*Large Green.*
10½ Early Violet, *twice bearing.*	26 Malta.	41½ Verte petite.
11 ‡Entire leaved.	27 Meziek's Favorite, *yellow, pear-shaped.*	42 ‡White Genoa, *large.*
12 Franque Pailarde.		43 ‡Yellow, or Golden.
		44 Violette de Bordeaux.
		45 Ronde Violette native.

POMEGRANATES—GRENADIERS.

This fruit requires in this latitude that the trees should be well bound with straw, or have a temporary frame of boards over them. All produce fruit except the double flowering varieties.

1 Fruit bearing	$0 50	10 White flowering and fruited	75
2 Large Malta	1 00	11 Double white flowering	75
3 Algiers Sweet froited	1 50	12 Yellow flowering do., with yellow fruit	75
4 Spanish	1 50	13 Double yellow flowering	1 00
5 Desportes, or Hybrida	1 50	14 Dwarf profuse flowering, Fruit bearing	50
6 Provence, *large fruit*	1 50	15 Large seedless	1 50
7 Double Crimson	50	16 Chinese double variegated, scarlet and white, large and splendid	1 50
8 Royal double Crimson (Regalis)	1 00		
9 Prolific	1 50	17 Desfontaines, *fine fruit*	1 50

3

RASPBERRIES—FRAMBOISIERS.

All the varieties are red except those designated otherwise, and all mature their fruit in July except the Twice Bearing kinds, and they produce a second crop in September or October. In order to have an ample crop of autumnal fruit, it is necessary to prune off the old shoots entirely in February or beginning of March, as the autumnal fruit is produced entirely on the shoots of the same year. There are no Monthly Raspberries; but only Twice Bearing ones. The leading varieties can be supplied by the hundred or thousand at reduced rates.—N. B. Any number less than a dozen will be charged higher.

	Per Doz.	Per 100.
1 American Red Prolific—English Red erroneously, fine flavor, very productive, long red shoots, never winter-killed.	1 25	8 00
2 American Red Cluster, very hardy.	1 00	6 00
3 American Black Cap—Doolittle's Improved Black Cap.	75	4 00
4 American White Cap, similar in quality to Black Cap.	1 50	10 00
5 Allen's Prolific — Red Cane, long red canes, very hardy.	75	5 00
6 Antwerp, Hudson River Red, large conical, suitable for market, short canes.	60	3 50
Do. per 1,000, $20; per 10,000, $150.		
7 Antwerp, Red, tall canes, nearly spineless, fruit longer than preceding, unsurpassed, requires winter protection. But few Nurseries possess this genuine variety.	1 50	10 00
8 Antwerp, Brentford Red, ovate, large, estimable, hardiest of large Raspberries.	2 00	12 00
9 Antwerp, Globose Red, firm for market, very large, roundish, excellent, bright crimson, robust, very productive, one of the hardiest, bears some fruit in autumn, a great acquisition. N. B.—If the old canes are pruned short in March, it will bear fruit throughout the summer.	2 00	12 00
10 Antwerp, Yellow or White, large, conical, pale yellow, excellent flavor, requires winter protection.	75	5 00
11 Bagley's Perpetual, very hardy, medium, round, dull crimson, fair crop in July, and large autumnal crop on young canes.	1 00	7 00
12 Belle de Fontenay, twice bearing, dark crimson, ovate, very large, second crop in Sep'r.	1 75	10 00
13 Belle de Palluau, red, large, fine.	2 00	14 00
14 Black Hybrid, Rivers, medium size, very acid, hardy.	2 00	12 00
15 Cæsar rouge, large, good.	2 50	
16 Californian Salmonberry, large, estimable, very hardy.	6 00	
17 Canadian Red, musk flavor, hardy, succeeds best at the north.	1 50	10 00
18 Carter's Prolific, large, good.	3 00	
19 Catawissa, dark red, twice bearing, hardy, large crop from August to October.	2 50	16 00
20 Chilian Red, large, late, acidulous.	2 50	16 00
21 Chilian Yellow, large, orange, good.	2 00	12 00
22 Columbia, yellow, medium size, twice bearing, fine flavor, new.	5 00	
Col. Wilder, see Wilder.		
24 Cope, light red, ovate, largest of all, productive, very valuable.	2 50	16 00
25 Coral Cluster, medium size, bright red, hardy, roundish, excellent flavor, in clusters, estimable, very productive.	1 50	10 00
26 Crimson Perpetual Antwerp, ovate, large, fine flavor, exceedingly productive, vigorous, estimable.	5 00	
27 Cushing, crimson, ovate, sprightly flavor, very productive, twice bearing, estimable.	1 50	8 00
28 Fastolf, red, large, estimable.	1 00	7 00
29 Fastolf Perpetual, large, crimson, crop in autumn.	2 00	12 00
30 Fastolf Seedling, large, red, fine.	2 50	15 00
31 Fillbasket, large red.	1 50	
32 Fouette perpetuelle, (New French variety).	2 00	
33 Four Seasons, red, twice bearing.	2 00	12 00
34 Franconia, rather large, productive, dark red, hardy.	1 00	6 00
35 French (Brinckle), crimson, roundish, very productive, rather large, good flavor.	1 50	8 00
36 Hornet, large red.	3 00	
37 Imperial White, large.	2 50	
38 Kirtland, red, medium, very hardy, twice bearing.	75	4 00
39 Knevett's Giant, deep red, obtuse cone, large, firm, productive, vigorous.	1 50	10 00
40 Large Monthly (Rivers), red, good flavor, very productive, good autumnal crop.	1 50	10 00
41 Magnum Bonum, medium size, straw color, round, hardy.	1 25	6 00
42 Merveille des quatre saisons, bright crimson, very large, ovate, twice bearing, large autumnal crop.	2 50	12 00
43 Merveille des quatre saisons, yellow, large, beautiful, oval, twice bearing, profuse autumnal crop.	6 00	
44 Monticello Cluster, red, productive, cool shady position, succeeds best at the north.	1 00	7 00
45 Ohio Twice-Bearing (Black Cap), large autumnal crop.	2 50	15 00

46 Orange (Brinckle), large, firm, estimable for market, productive......1 50	8 00	53 Walker, large, round, deep red, firm, good.................2 00	12 00
47 Richardson, large crimson, ovate, hardy, productive, valuable....2 50	16 00	54 White Prolific, excellent flavor, very hardy, in cluster, cool shady position, often twice bearing.................2 00	12 00
48 Souchette, new French variety.2 00		55 White Smooth Cane, almost spineless..................2 00	12 00
49 Superb English, red, large, vigorous...................2 50	16 00	56 Wilder, pale buff, roundish, productive, only moderate flavor...1 00	7 00
50 Surprise, a variety of Black Cap.		57 Yorkshire, red, smooth cane...1 50	10 00
51 Thunderer, large red, productive, rather acid, estimable....2 00	8 00	58 Yellow Globe...............1 25	6 00
52 Turban, red................1 50			

N. B.—For Flowering Varieties, see Ornamental Shrubs.

RASPBERRIES—*Varieties superseded or Synonyms.*

Barnet.	Nottingham Scarlet.	Wilmot's Early Red.
Cretan Red.	Perpetual White, *synonym.*	Woodward.
Double Bearing.	Twice Bearing.	Woodward's Red Globe.
Magnum Bonum, *red.*	Victoria (Cornwallis).	

CURRANTS—GROSEILLER À GRAPPES.

Any number less than 6 will be charged at the retail price; and any number between 6 and 12 will be charged intermediate between the retail and the dozen prices. When wanted by 100 or 1000, they will be supplied at very reduced rates. Extra large sized bushes, 3 and 4 years old, can be supplied at a moderate advance in price.

	Each.	Dozen.		Each.	Dozes.
1 Attrocar, or Attractor, *white, large, productive, peculiar foliage* (? syn.).............	38	4 00	17 Gloire des Sablons, *berries striped white and red, extra quality*...................	1 00	
2 Belle de Fontenay, *new*.....	50	4 50	18 Gondoin, Red, *medium, very acid*...................	25	2 50
3 Belle de St. Gilles, *new*.....	50	5 00	19 Gondoin, White, *rather large, mild acid*...............	25	2 50
4 Bang-up Black, *largest black.*	25	2 50	20 Hative de Bertia, *large early, deep red, mild, first quality, long cluster, very beautiful, translucent, one of the finest.*	50	4 50
5 Black Naples, or Black Grape, *large, productive*..........	15	1 50	21 Imperial Rouge, *large; long cluster*..................	50	5 00
6 Black English, *inferior, rejected.*			22 Imperial Jaune, *large, long cluster*.................	75	8 00
N. B.—*The three last-named varieties are used for liquers, medicinal conserves, and jellies, and by some for dessert.*			23 Knight's Early Red, *medium, resembles Red Dutch*.......	25	2 50
7 Black Maple-leaved........	38	3 50	24 Knight's Large Red, *larger than Red Dutch*.........	25	2 50
8 Black Variegated-leaved....	25		25 Knight's Sweet Red, *mild acid, long cluster, productive, size of Red Dutch*........	18	1 75
9 Brown-fruited (variety of Black).................	25	2 50	26 La Caucase, *red, very large, long cluster, mild acid. The genuine is yet rare*........	50	5 00
10 Boulogne, Large Red.......	75	6 00	27 La Fertile, *deep red, very productive*...............	20	2 00
11 Boulogne, Large White.....	75	6 00	28 La Hative, *red, early*.......	20	2 00
12 Champagne, *medium size, flesh color, transparent, sharp acid, hangs late, estimable*......	15	1 50	29 Lovett's Seedling, *red*.......	25	2 50
13 Cherry—Cerise, or Cerise de Tours, *very large, deep red, not too acid, beautiful, estimable*............	25	2 50	30 Macrocarpa, *large, supposed synonym*...............	38	3 50
Ditto, per 100, $18 to $25, according to age.			31 Magnum Bonum, *medium, very productive, resembles Red Dutch*............	20	1 75
Ditto, 2 and 3 years, larger size............	38	4 00	32 Maple-leaved Red..........	50	4 50
14 Cherry Long-bunched — Cerise à longue grappes......	50	5 00	33 Missouri Fragrant Yellow-flowering, *large, round, compressed, black, shining fruit, astringent*...............	18	2 00
De Hollande, *is Dutch, either red or white.*			34 Missouri Sweet-fruited, *oval, blue, late*.................	18	1 38
15 Fertile d'Angers, *red, large, next to Cherry in size, excellent flavor, very productive, estimable*................	50	4 50			
16 Fertile Precoce de Palluau, *red, large, early, very mild, excellent, beautiful, very productive*................	25	2 00			
Ditto, larger sized plants....	38	4 00			

35 Missouri Scentless Yellow, round yellow fruit	25	2 50
36 Missouri Golden, large, sweet, pleasant	50	4 50
37 Prince Albert, rather large, light red, very productive, late, estimable	38	4 00
38 Prince's Albiness, large, white, transparent, mild	1 00	10 00
39 Prince's Coral, large, red, beautiful, very productive, excellent	1 00	10 00
40 Red Dutch Long-bunched, rather large, long cluster, full acid, fine flavor, productive, hangs late	12	1 00
Red Grape, the ordinary kind is Red Dutch		
41 Red Grape (true), rather large, long cluster, too acid	20	2 00
42 Red Provence, medium size, light red, long cluster, sharp acid, productive, large foliage, young shoots blood-red N. B.—The Red Dutch is usually sold for this very distinct and rare variety	20	2 25
43 Short-bunched Red Dutch, medium size, good, vigorous	18	2 00
44 Striped leaved White	50	4 00
45 Superb Grape, red, very large, beautiful, next to Cherry in size, productive, very valuable	38	4 00
46 Transparent White, or White Grape, large, amber, rather		
mild, beautiful, very productive, hangs late	25	2 00
Ditto, larger plants	38	4 00
47 Variegated leaved, or Silver striped, red berries	20	2 00
48 Versaillaise, red, next to Cherry in size, longer cluster, beautiful, very productive, hangs late	25 to 38	3 to 4
Ditto, larger plants	50	4 50
49 Victoria, or Goliath, medium size, bright red, long cluster, hangs late, productive, estimable	20	2 00
White Antwerp, White Clinton, White Crystal, } are White Dutch.		
50 White Chasselas	25	2 50
51 White Dutch, medium size, mild, long cluster, pleasant flavor	12	1 50
White Grape (Rivers), Spurious, Rejected		
White Grape, see Transparent White		
52 White Pearl, La Perlé	15	1 50
53 White Provence, largest of Whites, as large as the Cherry, mildest of all, silver edged leaves, an extraordinary variety of great value	50	4 50
54 Wilmot's Grape, medium size, red, productive, probably a synonym	20	1 75
55 Yellow Champagne,—Synonym?	38	4 00

☞ *We have a number of New White and Red Seedlings, which we shall offer next year.*
N. B.--Flowering Currants, see Ornamental Shrubs.

GOOSEBERRIES–GROSEILLERS EPINEUX.

150 Largest and finest Lancashire varieties. Select kinds by name, 20 cents each—$2 per dozen. Extra large plants 3 and 4 years old, 25 cents, $2 50 per dozen. English ordinary Varieties, 15 cents, $1 50 per dozen.

The present selection has been made in accordance with the London Horticultural Society and others, and comprises only such as they have recommended after 25 years' experience.

N. B.—Directions will be given that will entirely prevent mildew.

Red. Atlas, Beauty of England, British Crown, Champagne red, Companion, Coronation, Crown Bob, Drum major, Elijah, Emperor, Farmer's Glory, Huntsman, Ironmonger, Keen's Seedling, Lancashire lad, Magistrate, Marquis of Stafford, Miss Bold, Napoleon, Overall, Pastime, Ploughboy, Plumber, Prince Regent, Printer, Rifleman, Ringleader, Royal George, Royal Oak, Roaring Lion, Shakespeare, Sportsman, Steward, Triumphant, Warrington, Warrior, Victory.

White. Bonny Lass, Champagne white, Cheshire Lass, Chorister, Cossack, Fleur de lis, Governess, Lady of Manor, Liberty, Lion-ess, Ostrich, Queen Anne, Sheba Queen, Victoria, Wellington, Whitesmith, White Eagle, White Lion.

Yellow. Bunker Hill, Champion, Early Sulphur, Golden drop, Golden gourd, Golden fleece, Hero, Husbandman, Leader, Liberator, Prince of Orange, Regulator, Teazer, Trueman, Viper, Yellow ball.

Green. Brougham, Faithful, Favorite, Gascoigne, Glenton, Governor, Greenwalnut, Greenwood, Heart of Oak, Independent, Jolly Angler, Keepsake Laurel, Lord Crew, Ne plus ultra, Nobleman, Perfection, Thumper, Zenith.

American Varieties, which never mildew. Houghton Red, 20 cents and $2 per dozen, $12 per 100. Houghton Crimson, 25 cents and $2 50 per dozen. Houghton Purple, 25 cents and $2 50 per dozen. Downing's Cluster, *greenish white*, 38 cents. Foster's Seedling, 50 cents. Mountain Seedling, purple, 25 cents and $2 50 per dozen. Prince's Cluster, *new*, 50 cents. Smith's White, 50 cents.

BLACKBERRIES.

	Dozen.	Hundred.
1 Trailing Dewberry, *sweet, large*	1 00	6 00
2 High Bush, or Standing, *oval, late*	1 00	6 00
3 Whitish, or Buff, *profuse bearer*	2 00	12 00
4 Dorchester (high bush), *large, firm, sweet*	1 50	8 00
5 New Rochelle, or Lawton, *extra large, estimable*	1 50	8 00
6 Parsley leaved, or Late Pro lific, *large, sweet, aromatic flavor, ripening after Law ton, very productive, estim able, rare*	3 50	25 00

	Dozen.	Hundred.
7 Mulberry	2 00	
8 Crystal White, *large, fine fla vor*	1 00	
9 Kentucky White	3 00	
10 Hartshorn, *very long fruited*	3 00	
11 Alpine, *climbing, in clusters*	3 00	
12 Orange, *very large, dark brown, excellent*	2 00	12 00
13 Californian Sweet, *for the South*	4 50	
14 Mexican Alpine, *for the South*	1 50	
15 Newman's Thornless, *small berry*	2 00	

N. B.—For Flowering Brambles, see Vines and Creepers.

WHORTLEBERRIES, BERBERRIES, AND CRAN-BERRIES.

1 Whortleberry, or Huckleberry, Black, Blue, White, and others	20
2 Ditto per 100	12 00
3 Red fruited Berberry	20
4 Purple fruited and Purple leaved	40
5 White, or Yellow do	50
6 Sweet, or Dulcis do	25
7 Chinese red fruited, and Hybrid	38

N. B.—For other Berberries, see Ornamental Shrubs.

Round Cranberry, for lowland, per 200 $1, per 1000 $5, 5000 for $20, 10,000 for $30. | Bugle or Bell Cranberry, can be cultivated on upland. Same price as preceding.

High bush Cranberry, 25 to 38 cents each.

GRAPES.

A Descriptive Catalogue is published comprising all the finest European and American Varieties.

STRAWBERRIES.

A Descriptive Catalogue is published comprising Select Assortments of the most splendid and estimable American and European Varieties, with a *Rejected List*, and Directions for Culture, etc.

ESCULENT ROOTS, ETC.

1 Asparagus, Giant and Dutch, 1 to 3 years old, per hundred	50 to 75
do and do do per thousand	$4 to $6
2 Asparagus, Large German, 1 to 3 years, per hundred	75 to $1
do do do per thousand	$7 to $8

	Dozen.	Hundred.
3 Asparagus, Lesher's Mammoth		1 00
4 Artichoke, Jerusalem	38	2 00
5 do Green Globe	2 50	
6 Chinese Potato, or Yam (Dios corea)		3 00
Do do, per 1000...$20		
7 Dyer's Madder	2 00	8 00
8 Earth Almond, or Chufa		50
9 Ginseng	2 00	10 00
10 Hop Vine	1 25	4 00
11 Horse Radish	1 25	4 00
12 Licorice	4 00	15 00
13 Patience Dock, *finest early greens*	1 00	4 00
14 Sea Kale	2 50	
15 Tarragon, *for spicing salads*	3 00	
16 Water Cress	50	2 00

RHUBARB.	Each.	Dozen.
17 Early Tobolsk	25	1 50
18 Myatt's Victoria	25	1 50
19 Linnæus	30	2 00
Ditto per 100, $8; per 1000, $50 to $60		
20 Wilmot's Early	20	1 75
21 Giant, and Colossal	25	2 00
22 Cahoon's Mammoth	50	4 00
23 Hawke's Champagne	75	5 00
24 Dalley's Scarlet Giant	50	3 00
25 Magnum Bonum	38	3 00
26 Schofield's Prince Albert	30	2 00
27 Marshall's Early Scarlet	38	3 00
28 Prince of Wales (Sangster)	50	3 00
29 Blood Royal	50	3 50
30 Scarlet Nonpareil	75	5 00

RHUBARB.

31 Randall's Early Prolific	50	3 00	Hybrid Varieties, from Lin-
32 Gray Eagle	50	3 00	næus, Victoria, and Prince
33 Mitchell's Prince Albert	50	3 50	Albert, $1 50 per dozen; $8
34 Early Prince Imperial	60	5 00	per 100.

Large Quantities of the finest kinds for Market plantations at very low rates.

EVERGREEN AND DECIDUOUS HEDGE PLANTS.

	PER 100	PER 1000		PER 100	PER 1000
1 Buckthorn, or Rhamnus	2 00	10 to 12	17 Red Cedar, 3 to 4 ft.	12 00	
Ditto, large size	5 00	30 00	20 Privet, or Prim, Italian	2 to 5	17 to 24
2 Hawthorn		8 00	21 ——— scions	1 50	10 00
3 Honey Locust, as in size	3 to 4	15 00	22 Euonymus, or Strawberry		
4 Locust, Yellow, as in size	4 to 6		tree	10 to 12	
5 Maclura, or Osage Orange,			23 Althea frutex, according to		
1 to 3 years		4 to 8	size	5 to 10	
6 Amer. Arbor Vitæ, 1 to 1½ ft	5 00	40 00	24 Althea frutex, cuttings	2 00	
Do. 2 to 2½ feet	8 00	60 00	25 Honeysuckle, Tartarian,		
7 American Arbor Vitæ,			cuttings	3 00	
grown in Nursery, 2 years'			26 do English fly, straw		
seedlings	10 00		colored, cuttings	3 00	
8 do 1 to 2 ft.	10 00		27 Deutzia scabra, cuttings	3 00	
9 do 1½ to 2 ft.	14 00		28 Syringa, different kinds,		
10 do 2 to 2½ ft.	16 00		cuttings	2 00	
11 do 3 ft.	20 00		29 Red and Purple Lilac pln'ts	12 00	
12 do 4 ft.	30 00		30 Spiræas, Assorted	10 00	
13 Chinese Arbor Vitæ, 1½ to 2 ft	18 00		31 Mahonia, 3 species	8 00	
14 Chinese Arbor Vitæ, 2 to 2½ ft	20 00		32 Tamarisk, several	9 00	
15 Hemlock, Spruce, 1 to 2½ ft.	12 00		33 Upright Honeysuckle	9 00	
16 Red Cedar, 1½ to 2 ft.	6 00		34 Norway Spruce	12 00	

PLANTS FOR EDGING BORDERS.

	PER YARD.		PER YARD.
1 Dwarf Box, cuttings or slips, pre-		7 Moss Pink	50
pared	10	8 Fragrant, and Tricolored Violet	50
2 Dwarf Box, rooted plants, according		9 Cowslip, Red and Yellow	75
to age and quantity	18 to 20	10 Vinca, Green and Variegated-leaved,	
3 Dwarf Box, rooted plants, 2 yrs. old	25	$6 per 100	50
4 do 3 and 4 years	38	11 Bush Alpine Strawberry, Red and	
5 Dwarf Iris, for edging borders	50	White	50
6 Thrift, or Sea Pink	50		

SCIONS FOR ENGRAFTING AND CUTTINGS.

Scions of all kinds of Fruit Trees, suitable for grafting, will be supplied when 40 or more kinds are ordered, more or less of each, as convenient to us, at 25 cents per parcel, or at 50 cents per dozen grafts of each variety where the price of a tree does not exceed that sum (50 cents); but where it does, the same price will be charged for the dozen scions, or for a parcel where the kind is very rare, as for a tree of the same kind. When a large number of scions are wanted, of the leading varieties, they will be supplied at $1 50 per 100, or at the following rates per 1000, all correctly *labeled*: Apples, $5, Pears, $6, Cherries, $6, Plums, $10.

Scions of Anger's Quince, for budding Pears on, $1 50 per 100, and $10 per 1000, and Scions of the plentiful kinds of Currants, Gooseberries, Raspberries, Berberries, Mulberries, Poplars, Willows, Altheas, Roses, and of all other Trees and Shrubs that will grow from cuttings, $2 50 per 100 and $20 per 1000, and Figs and Pomegranates $5 to $8 per 100; but no quantity is sent amounting to less than the price of a Tree or Shrub of the same kind. Scions of the eight finest species of Osiers, most celebrated for baskets, &c., $1 per 100 and $2 to $5 per 1000. It is better that such orders be sent in the fall or winter; and the scions can be forwarded by express if so ordered.

Scions of Grapes, of a number of the finest Foreign kinds, can be supplied if applied for in season, at from $4 to $8 per 100, or in less quantities; but in no case will scions of any variety be sent to a less amount than the price of a vine; and of the very rare varieties three scions or eyes, and of others six scions or eyes of any one variety will be considered equivalent in value to a vine. Scions of Isabella, Catawba, Clinton, and several other varieties of Grapes, $2 per 100, or $8 to $12 per 1000.

ORANGE, LEMON, CITRON, SHADDOCK, and LIME TREES, and all other GREEN HOUSE TREES and PLANTS, can be supplied at reasonable rates.

PREFERABLE DISTANCE FOR PLANTATIONS OF TREES.

Standard Apples—30 feet distant each way.
Standard Pears, and Cherries, 20 feet.
Standard Peaches, Plums, Apricots, and Nectarines, 12 feet.
Quinces, 8 to 10 feet.

Pyramidal Apples, Pears, Cherries, and Plums, and Dwarf Pears, 8 feet.
Dwarf Apples, 6 feet.
Gooseberries, and Currants, 3 to 4 feet.

The number of Trees requisite for an Acre, at certain distances.

4 Feet apart each way,	2722	16 Feet apart each way, 170
5 " " "	1742	20 " " " 109
6 " " "	1210	25 " " " 70
8 " " "	681	30 " " " 48
10 " " "	435	36 " " " 33
12 " " "	325	40 " " " 27
15 " " "	194	

SELECT FRUIT CATALOGUE, ADOPTED BY THE AMERICAN POMOLOGICAL SOCIETY.

At their Session held at New York, September, 1858.

APPLES—*for General Cultivation.*

American Summer Pearmain.
Autumn Bough.
Baldwin.
Benoni.
Bullock's Pippin.
Carolina June.
Danvers Winter Sweet.
Early Harvest.
Early Strawberry.
Fall Pippin.
Fameuse.
Gravenstein.

Hawley.
High Top Sweeting.
Hubbardston Nonsuch.
Jonathan.
Lady Apple.
Ladies' Sweet.
Large Yellow Bough.
Melon.
Minister.
Monmouth Pippin.
Porter.
Primate.

Rambo.
Red Astrachan.
Rhode Island Greening.
Roxbury Russett.
Smith's Cider.
Summer Rose.
Swaar.
Vandervere.
Wagener.
William's Favorite.
Wine or Hays.
Wine Sap.

APPLES—*which promise well.*

Broadwell.
Buckingham.
Coggswell.
Fornwalder.

Genessee Chief.
Jeffries.
King of Tompkins County.
Mother.

Smoke House.
White Winter Pearmain.
Winter Sweet Paradise.
Lincoln Pippin.

APPLES—*for Particular Localities.*

Canada Red.
Esopus Spitzenburgh.

Newtown Pippin.
Northern Spy.

Yellow Bellefleur.

PEARS—*for General Cultivation.* (*Standard.*)

Ananas d'Eté.
Andrews.
Bartlett.
Beurré d'Anjou.
Beurré d'Aremberg.
Beurré Diel.
Beurré Bose.
Beurré St. Nicholas.
Beurré Clairgeau.
Beurré Giffard.
Beurré Superfin.
Brandywine.
Bloodgood.
Buffum.

Cabot.
Dearborn's Seedling.
Doyenné d'Eté.
Doyenné Boussock.
Doyenné d'Alençon.
Flemish Beauty.
Fondante d'Automne.
Fulton.
Golden Beurré of Bilboa.
Kingsessing.
Howell.
Lawrence.
Louise Bonne de Jersey.
Madeleine.

Manning's Elizabeth.
Onondaga.
Osband's Summer.
Paradise d'Automne.
Rostiezer.
Seckel.
Shelden.
St. Michael Archange.
Tyson.
Urbaniste.
Vicar of Winkfield.
Winter Nelis.
Uvedale's St. Germain, (*for baking.*)

PEARS—*which promise well.*

Adams.
Alpha.
Bergen.
Beurré d'Albert.

Beurré gris d'hiver nouveau.
Beurré Hardy.
Beurré Kennes.
Beurré Langelier.

Beurré Nantais.
Chancellor.
Charles Van Hooghten.
Collins.

Comte de Flandres.
Conseiller de la Cour.
Comtesse d'Alost.
Dehors d'Hardempont de Bel-
  gique.
Dix.
Duc de Brabant.
Rousselette d'Esperen.
Sterling.
Theodore Van Mons.

Duchesse de Berri d'Eté.
Emile d'Heyst.
Fondante de Comice.
Fondante de Malines.
Fondante de Noel.
Henkel.
Hosen Schenk.
Hull.
Jalousie de Fontenay Vendée.
Kirtland.

Lodge.
Niles.
Ott.
Philadelphia.
Pinneo or Boston.
Pius IX.
Pratt.
Van Assche.
Walker.
Zepherin Gregoire.

PEARS—*for Particular Localities.* (*Standard.*)

Gray Doyenné.

White Doyenné.

PEARS—*for General Cultivation on the Quince Stock.*

Beurré Superfin.
Beurré Hardy.
Butfum.
Belle Epine Dumas.
Beurré d'Amanlis.
Beurré d'Anjou.
Beurré Diel.
Beurré Langelier.
Catillac.

Duchesse d'Angoulême.
Doyenné d'Alençon.
Easter Beurré.
Figue d'Alençon.
Fondante d'Automne.
Glout Morceau.
Louise Bonne de Jersey.
Napoleon.
Nouveau Poiteau.

Rostiezer.
Soldat Laboreur.
St. Michael Archange.
Urbaniste.
Uvedale's St. Germain, (*for bak-
  ing*)
Vicar of Winkfield.
White Doyenné.

PEACHES—*for General Cultivation.*

Bergen's Yellow.
Crawford's Early.
Crawford's Late.
Cooledge's Favorite.
Early York, *Serrate.*

Grosse Mignonne.
Morris White Rareripe.
Large Early York, or Geo. IV.
Hill's Chili.
Large White Cling.

Madeleine de Courson.
Teton de Venus.
Old Mixon Free.
Old Mixon Cling.

PEACHES—*which promise well.*

Gorgas.

Susquehanna.

PEACHES—*for Particular Localities.*

Chinese Cling.

Heath Cling.

Carpenter's White.

PLUMS—*for General Cultivation.*

Bleecker's Gage.
Coe's Golden Drop.
Green Gage.
Jefferson.
Lawrence's Favorite.

Lombard.
Monroe.
Purple Favorite.
Prince's Yellow Gage.
Purple Gage.

Reine Claude de Bavay.
Smith's Orleans.
Washington.
McLaughlin.

PLUMS—*which promise well.*

Bradshaw.
Duane's Purple.
Italian Prune.
General Hand.

German Prune.
Monroe.
Ive's Washington.
Pond's Seedling (English).

Rivers' Favorite.
St. Martin's Quetche.
White Damson.

PLUMS—*for Particular Localities.*
Imperial Gage.

CHERRIES—*for General Cultivation.*

Belle d'Orleans.
Belle Magnifique.
Black Eagle.
Black Tartarian.
Coe's Transparent.

Downer's Late.
Early Purple Guigne.
Governor Wood.
Elton.
Early Richmond (*for cooking*).

Graffion or Bigarrean.
Knight's Early Black.
May Duke.
Reine Hortense.

CHERRIES—*which promise well.*

American Amber.
Bigarreau de Mezel.
Black Hawk.

Large Prool, or Great Bigar-
  reau.
Rockport.
Hovey.

Kirtland's Mary.
Ohio Beauty.
Black Bigarreau of Savoy.

APRICOTS—*for General Cultivation.*

Breda.

Large Early.

Moorpark.

NECTARINES—*for General Cultivation.*

Downton.

Early Violet.

Elruge.

GRAPES—*for General Open Culture.*

Catawba.
Concord.

Delaware.

Diana.

GRAPES—*for Open Culture, which promise well.*

Herbemont.
Logan.

Rebecca.

Union Village.

GRAPES *under Glass.*

Black Damascus.
Black Hamburgh.
Black Frontignan.
Black Lombardy.
Black Prince.

Chasselas de Fontainbleau.
Red Chasselas.
Cannon Hall Muscat.
Grizzly Frontignan.

White Frontignan.
White Muscat of Alexandria.
White Nice.
Zinfardel or Zinfindal.

RASPBERRIES—*for General Cultivation.*

Fastolf.
Franconia.
French.

Knevett's Giant.
Orange.

Red Antwerp.
Yellow Antwerp.

RASPBERRIES—*which promise well.*

Cope.
Catawissa.

Thunderer.

Walker.

STRAWBERRIES—*for General Cultivation.*

Boston Pine.
Hovey's Seedling.
Burr's New Pine.

Longworth's Prolific.
Large Early Scarlet.

Hooker's Seedling.
Wilson's Albany.

STRAWBERRIES—*which promise well.*

Genesee.
Le Baron.

McAvoy's Superior.
Scarlet Magnate (Prince's).

Trollope's Victoria.
Walker's Seedling.

STRAWBERRIES—*for Particular Localities.*
Burr's New Pine.

CURRANTS—*for General Cultivation.*

Black Naples.
Victoria.

Red Dutch.
White Dutch.

Transparent White, or White
Grape.

CURRANTS—*which promise well.*

Versaillaise.

Cherry.

Fertile de Palluau.

GOOSEBERRIES—*for General Cultivation.*

Crown Bob.
Early Sulphur.
Green Gage.
Green Walnut.

Houghton's Seedling.
Ironmonger.
Laurel

Red Champagne.
Warrington.
Woodward's White Smith.

BLACKBERRIES—*for General Cultivation.*

New Rochelle, or Lawton.

Dorchester.

4

Ornamental Department.

SELECT DECIDUOUS ORNAMENTAL TREES.

THE following comprise a *Select Assortment* of the most beautiful and estimable species, which our long experience has enabled us to arrange with precision. The inferior species we have omitted.

We have divided them into four classes. The first class comprises those of majestic growth, which attain great stature and ample development ; the second class, those which attain a medium size ; the third class, those of low stature ; and the fourth class, such as are comparatively of slow growth, requiring a long period before they attain the size of a small tree, and which, therefore, it would be more appropriate, in ornamenting grounds, to rank among large Shrubs.

The prices stated are for trees of fair size ; but where extra large-sized trees are desired for Streets, Avenues, &c., in order to impart immediate ornament, such can be supplied at proportionate rates, varying in height from ten to twenty feet, of many of the most estimable species.

Botanical Name.	Common Name.	Class.	Price.
Acer.	**Maple.**		
1 Acer dasycarpum	Silvery-leaved	1	35 to 50
	Ditto, large, 12 to 14 feet	1	75 to 1 00
3 Acer macrophyllum	Oregon	1	50
4 Acer platanoides	Norway	1	35 to 50
5 Acer vari gata	Silver striped leaved	3	1 00
6 Acer rubrum	Scarlet flowering	2	35 to 50
7 Acer saccharinum	Sugar, Hard, or Rock	1	50
8 Acer striatum	Striped bark	2	50
9 Acer pseudoplatanus	European Syeamore	1	50
10 Acer argen, varieg. and 8 other species	Striped-leaved do	4	75
	Horse Chestnut.		
11 Aesculus flava	Yellow flowering	2	50
12 Aesculus glabra	Green do	2	50
13 Aesculus hippocastanum	White, or Variegated flowering	1	35 to 50
14 Aesculus flore pleno	Double flowering, *splendid and rare*	2	1 50
15 Aesculus pavia vel coccinea	Scarlet do	4	1 00
16 Aesculus rubicunda	Coral colored	2	1 00
17 Aesculus pallida, dark glossy foliage, holds it late pale yellow flowers, lofty	Ohio Buckeye	1	75
18 Ailanthus glandulosa	Ailanthus, Chinese	1	50
19 Alnus incana	Alder, European Silvery	1	50
20 Alnus laciniata	Alder, Cut-leaved	2	75
21 Amygdalus communis	Almond, Flowering (See page 24)		38 to 50
22 Amygdalus persica	Peach, Flowering (See page 26)		38 to 50
23 Aralia spinosa	Prickly Ash, or Hercules' club	2	38
24 Aralia japonica	Japan do , unique and showy	2	40 to 75
25 Betula alba pendula	Birch, Scotch drooping	1	50
26 Betula laciniata	Birch, Cut-leaved	3	40
27 Broussonetia papyrifera	Paper Mulberry	2	30 to 50
28 Carya	Hickory Nut. (See page 24)		
29 Castanea	Chestnut. (See page 24.)		
30 Catalpa syringefolia	Catalpa, Variegated flowers	1	38
31 Catalpa Daytoni	Catalpa, Dayton, new	1	75
32 Catalpa Bungeana	Catalpa, Chinese, *beautiful.*	2	1 00
33 Catalpa Kempferi	Catalpa, Kempfer's Japan, new	2	1 00
34 Cerasus	Cherry, Double Flowering. (See page 11.)		
35 Cerasus padus	Cherry, European Bird, beautiful	3	50
36 Cercis canadensis	Judas tree, American	2	38
37 Cercis siliquastrum	Judas tree, European	4	50
38 Cercis alboa	Judas tree, White flowering	4	1 00

	Botanical Name	Common Name.	Class.	Price.
40	Chionanthus virginica..	Fringe tree, White, *broad leaved*.	3	38 to 1 00
41	Chionanthus maritima	Fringe tree, Carolina, *narrow leaved*..	5	38 to 1 00
41½	Clethra arborea	Tree Clethra.	2	1 00
42	Cornus florida	Dogwood, White flowering	2	25
43	Crataegus	Hawthorn. (See Deciduous Ornamental Shrubs.)		
44	Cytisus laburnum	Laburnum, or Golden chain	3	25 to 50
45	Cytisus alpinus	Laburnum, Scotch, large flowering	3	25 to 50
46	Cytisus purpureum	Laburnum, Purple flowering	6	75
48	Diospyros.	Persimon. (See page 25).		
49	Eleagnus angustifolius	Silvery Bohemian Olive	2	1 00
50	Fagus ferruginea	Beech, American	1	50
51	Fagus sylvatica	Beech, European	2	25
52	Fagus *purpurea*	Beech, Purple leaved	2	75 to 1 00
55	Fraxinus atrovirens crispa	Ash, Curl-leaved, *curious*.	3	75
56	Fraxinus aurea	Ash, Gold bark	2	75
58	Fraxinus excelsior	Ash, European, rapid growth	1	25 to 50
61	Fraxinus platycarpa	Ash, Carolina	2	50
63	Fraxinus sambucifolia	Ash, Black	1	50
64	Fraxinus viridis	Ash, Green	3	75
65	Gleditschia triacanthos	Honey Locust	1	25 to 38
66	Gleditschia sinensis	Chinese do	2	50
67	Gymnocladus canadensis	Kentucky Coffee	2	30 to 50
68	Halesia. (See Deciduous Ornam'l Shrubs).			
69	Juglans	Walnut. (See page 24).		
70	Koelreuteria paniculata	Koelreuteria, Japan panicled	2	38
71	Larix europea	Larch, European Drooping	1	25 to 50
72	Larix tyrolosa	Larch, Tyrolese		60
73	Larix Microcarpa	Larch, American	2	25
74	Laurus sassafras	Sassafras	2	25
75	Liquidamber styraciflua	Sweet Gum, Maple leaved	1	50
76	Liriodendron tulipifera	Tulip tree, or Whitewood	1	30 to 50
77	Maclura aurantiaca	Osage Orange, male and female	2	25
78	Magnolia acuminata	Magnolia, Blue flowering	1	50
79	Magnolia auriculata	Magnolia, Auriculate, white fragrant.	2	1 to 2 00
80	Magnolia conspicua	Magnolia, Chinese splendid White...	2	1 to 2 00
		Ditto, large and splendid trees 6 to 10 feet		5 to 10 00
81	Magnolia *Alexandrina*	Magnolia, Alexandrian, Crimson striped, twice blooming	3	1 50 to 3 00
82	Magnolia *amabilis*	Lovely, white fragrant	3	5 00
83	Magnolia *Norbertiana*	Magnolia, Norbert's, deep striped	3	2 to 3 00
84	Magnolia *Soulangiana*	Magnolia, Soulange's Pink striped	3	1 to 2 00
85	Magnolia *Speciosa*. or *Striata*	Magnolia, Splendid striped	3	1 50 to 2 00
86	Magnolia *Superba*	Magnolia, Superb striped	3	1 50 to 2 00
87	Magnolia longifolia	Long leaved Glaucous	2	1 00

N. B.—The above five Magnolias are twice flowering.

88	Magnolia cordata biflora	Magnolia, Yellow twice-flowering....	2	1 00 to 2 00
89	Magnolia glauca	Magnolia, Glaucous Fragrant	2	30 to 50
90	Magnolia macrophylla	Magnolia, Largest flowered, white, crimson center	2	1 to 2 00
		Do do, splendid trees, 6 to 10 feet		3 to 6 00
91	Magnolia tripetela	Magnolia, Umbrella-leaved	2	50

N. B.—Extra large Magnolia trees at proportionate prices.
N. B.—For other Magnolias, see Deciduous Ornamental Shrubs, and Evergreens.

92	Melia azederach	Pride of India	2	1 00
92½	Mespilus	Medlar. (See page 25).		
93	Morus	Mulberry. (See page 24).		
93½	Negundo fraxinifolia	Negundo, Ash leaved	2	38
94	Negundo violacea	Negundo, Californian Violet	2	1 00
95	Ornus europeus	Ornus, or White fringe	2	50
96	Ornus latifolia	Ornus, Broad-leaved Fringe	2	1 00
97	Ostrya virginica	Hoptree	2	50
98	Paulownia imperialis	Paulownia, Imperial	2	50 to 75
99	Platanus occidentalis	Buttonwood, or Sycamore	1	30
100	Platanus orientalis	Oriental Plane	1	30 to 50

Botanical Name.	Common Name.	Class.	Price.
101 Platanus Californica...............	California Clustered-balled Plane....	1	1 00
102 Populus auriplia,...................	Abele, Snowy Maple-leaved..........	1	50
103 Populus balsamifera,...............	Poplar, Balsam, or Tacmahac.......	1	80
104 Populus fastigiata.................	Poplar, Lombardy...................	1	30
105 Populus grava.....................	Poplar, Athenian	1	50
106 Populus grandidentata.............	Poplar, Great Dentated	1	50
107 Populus lævigata..................	Poplar, Cotton tree, very lofty, broad-leaved, splendid foliage........	1	50 to 1 00
108 Populus tremula..................	Poplar, European Aspen............	1	30
110 Prunus...........................	Plum, Double flowering. (See p. 16).		
111 Pyrus or Sorbus Americana..........	Mountain Ash, American............	2	30 to 50
112 Pyrus aucuparia,.................	Mountain Ash, European.	2	25 to 50
113 Pyrus fructa aurea...............	Mountain Ash, Gold-n fruited.......	2	50
114 Pyrus Domestica.................	Service tree, or Sorb..............	2	50
	Apple, Double flowering. (See page 1).		
114½ Pyrus communispleno,.............	Pear, do do.		
115 Quercus Cerris...................	Oak, Turkey......................	2	25 to 50
116 Quercus Californica,.............	Oak, Californian Colossal..........	1	2 00
117 Quercus laurifolia,..............	Oak, Laurel-leaved................	1	1 00
118 Quercus Lucombeana,............	Oak, Lucombe's...................	3	1 00
118½ Quercus macrocarpa,.............	Oak, Mossy cup...................	1	25 to 50
119 Quercus pedunculairis.............	Oak, Long peduncled..............	1	1 00
120 Quercus phellos	Oak, Willow-leaved...............	1	50
121 Quercus robur,..................	Oak, English Royal	1	25

N. B.—A Collection of American Oaks at low rates by 100.

123 Rhus cotinus......................	Purple Fringe, Smoke tree, or Jupiter's beard.............	3	50
124 Robinia pseudacacia..............	Yellow Locust....................	1	25
125 Robinia viscosa,.................	Acacia, Blush flowering...........	3	35
126 Robinia spectabilis..............	Acacia, White do	2	75
127 Salisburia adiantifolia.............	Japan Gingko tree, splendid, with very unique foliage and of rapid growth	1	1 00
	Ditto, Extra Large, 4 to 15 feet..		2 to 10 00
128 Salix alba.......................	Willow, White or Huntingdon.......	1	38
129 Salix argentis,..................	Willow, Californian Silvery........	2	1 00
Salix Babylonica, see Weeping Trees.			
130 Salix capreapendula.............	Weeping Goat Willow.............	3	1 00
131 Salix purpurea..................	Willow, Purplish twigged..........	2	25
132 Salix Sacramentis,..............	Willow, Californian Broad-leaved,...	1	1 00
133 Salix vitellina..................	Willow, Golden...	1	20
134 Salix............................	Willow, Comewell, a good Osier,....	2	25

N. B.—For other Willows, see Osiers.

135 Sophora japonica..................	Sophora, Japan....................	3	50
137 Taxodium distichum..............	Cypress, American................	1	25 to 50
138 Taxodium sinensis................	Cypress, Chinese.................	1	1 00
139 Tilia Americana.................	Linden, American Basswood,........	1	40
140 Tilia argentea,.................	Linden, Silvery-leaved............	1	75 to 1 00
142 Tilia aurea,....................	Linden, Golden twigged...........	1	38 to 75
143 Tilia heterophylla,..............	Linden, Maple, or Cut-leaved......	2	75
144 Tilia macrophylla,..............	Linden, Umbrella-leaved..........	1	50 to 1 00
145 Tilia platyphylla,..............	Linden, European................	1	50
146 Tilia rubra,....................	Linden, Red-twigged.............	1	38 to 1 00
147 Ulmus Americana,..............	Elm, American Weeping...........	1	10 to 75
148 Ulmus campestris,..............	Elm, English pyramidal...........	1	38
151 Ulmus fulva....................	Elm, Red, or Slippery............	1	50
152 Ulmus montana,................	Elm, Scotch, or Wych............	1	38
154 Ulmus suberosa,................	Elm, Dutch Cork-barked...........	1	50

N. B.—Twelve other varieties can be supplied.

155 Virgilia lutea,..................	Yellow-wooded Virgilia...........	2	1 00

SELECTIONS OF ORNAMENTAL TREES, ETC.

The Trees most suitable for planting in Streets and Avenues are the Silver, Norway, and Sugar Maples, European Sycamore, the various Elms, Ohio Buckeye, with dark glossy foliage, Paulownia, Oriental Plane, Snowy Abele, the beautiful Salisburia of Japan, Tulip tree, Magnolia acuminata and maxima, American Cypress, European Ash, Red-twig Linden, and Silver leaved Linden.

The common variety of European Linden, and the common Horse Chestnut, drop their foliage so early in autumn that they are entirely unsuited for streets, but will answer for other locations. The Catalpa forms too spreading and irregular a head for planting in streets. The European Alder will best suit any wet locality. The Ailanthus has latterly fallen into disrepute on account of the odor of its blossoms; an evil easily remedied, however, by proper selection, as the odor proceeds only from one sex, latterly introduced, and therefore this objection does not apply at all to the tree originally introduced, which was of the other sex.

All the above-named trees are appropriate for extensive Lawns, to which may be added the Weeping Willow, one of the most elegant and graceful of all trees, and the Ring-leaved Weeping, the Huntingdon Green, and the Golden bark and Silvery leaved Willows to aid in the picturesque. The Liquidamber and Scarlet Maple are desirable not only for general ornament, but for their reddening foliage in early Autumn, thereby imparting a most pleasing diversity. The trees I have enumerated are not suitable for ordinary small yards and other circumscribed positions; and for that object, we should select trees of secondary stature, such as the Mountain Ash, Magnolia tripetela, Macrophylla, and Auriculata, White Fringed Ornus, Laburnum, Japan Angelica, European Bird Cherry, Blush Acacia, and Virgilia lutea.

We come next to the third Class of Trees, which may be more properly ranked as large Shrubs, as they branch low, and to the largest class of Flowering Shrubs, all of which may be pruned to suit the space to be occupied; such as the Magnolia Norbertiana, beautifully striped, the M. Soulangiana with paler stripes, M. Glauca and Conspicua with white flowers, and the Japan Purple, and Chinese Purple and White Flowering, the Halesia, Purple Fringe, Japan Sophora, Hawthorn, Cornelian Cherry, Silvery Eleagnus, European Euonymus, the beautiful varieties of Double Althea, Rhamnus carolinus, &c. These will serve to fill up the complement in adornment.

WEEPING TREES OF FAIR SIZE.

Ash, Weeping European	$1 00	Laburnum, Weeping	1 25
——, Weeping Asiatic	1 50	Larch, Scotch Drooping, *best*	1 50
——, Weeping Golden	1 50	——, Pendulous	2 00
Aspen, Weeping	1 00	Linden, Silvery Weeping	1 50
Beech, Weeping Green	1 50	Mountain Ash, Weeping	1 00
——, Weeping Purple	1 50	Peach, Weeping	60
Birch, Weeping Scotch	1 00	Pear, Weeping	75
——, Weeping Laciniate	1 00	Poplar, Weeping	75
Cherry, Weeping, *one of the most beautiful* $1 to $2		Sophora, Weeping	2 00
Cypress, Weeping	2 00	Willow, Weeping green	50
Cytisus, Weeping, 2 species	1 00	——, Weeping Ring-leaved	75
Elm, American Weeping	1 00	——, Kilmarnock Weeping	1 00
——, European Weeping	1 00	Robinia, Weeping	1 00

DECIDUOUS ORNAMENTAL SHRUBS.

The following comprises a *Select Assortment* of the most beautiful and estimable species. The inferior species are omitted. N. B.—Extra large Shrubs of most of the kinds can be supplied at proportionate prices.

Botanical Name.	Common Name.	Price.
1 Acacia Julibrissin	Sensitive tree	40 to 75
2 Amelanchier botryapium	Mespilus, Snowy flowered	38
3 Amelanchier arbutifolia	Mespilus, Scarlet-berried	50
4 Amorpha fruticosa	Indigo Shrub	25
5 Amorpha canescens	Indigo Shrub, Hoary	25
6 Amygdalus	Almond, Flowering. (See page 24.)	
7 Andromeda paniculata	Andromeda, panicled	50
8 Andromeda racemosa	Andromeda, Racemed	50
9 Andromeda pulverulenta	Andromeda, Splendid, and others	75
10 Artemesia abrotanum	Southernwood, or Citronelle	25

Botanical Name.	Common Name.	Price.
15 Azalea nudiflora	Azalea, Pink colored	38
16 Azalea viscosa	Azalea, White fragrant	50
17 Azalea Californica	Azalea, Californian	2 00
18 Azalea aurantiaca	Azalea, Orange colored	1 00
19 Azalea Belgica	Azalea, Belgic, of 30 splendid named varieties, $9 per dozen	75 to 1 00
20 Azalea coccinea major	Azalea, large Scarlet	1 00
21 Azalea Calendulacea	Azalea, Calendulacea, 12 splendid varieties	50 to 1 00
22 Azalea tricolor	Azalea, Tricolored	1 00
23 Azalea Pontica	Azalea, Pontic Yellow	50
24 Azalea do	Azalea, Pontic, 6 fine varieties	75

N. B.—A Special List of the Collection of Azalas will be sent to Amateurs.

25 **Baccharis** halimifolia	Snow drift tree	50
26 **Benthamia** fragrifera	Benthamia, Strawberry fruited	75
27 **Berberis** emarginata	Berberry, Marginate	50
28 Berberis nepalensis	Berberry, Nepal	25
29 Berberis sibirica	Berberry, Siberian	50
30 Berberis wallichiana	Berberry, Wallich's	25

N. B.—See other Species, page 29, and among Evergreen Shrubs.

31 **Borya** ligustrina	Borya, Privet leaved	60
32 Borya acuminata	Borya, Acuminate	50
33 **Buddlea** Lindleyana	Buddlea, Lindley's	25
34 **Callicarpa** japonica	Callicarpa, Japan	75
35 **Calycanthus** laevigatus	Sweet-scented Shrub, purple	25
	Ditto, larger size	50
36 Calycanthus floridus	Sweet-scented shrub, Downy-brown flow'd	25
37 Calycanthus glaucus	Sweet-scented shrub, Glaucous-leaved Red	25
38 Calycanthus Pennsylvanicus	Sweet-scented shrub, Pennsylvanian purple	38
39 Calycanthus semperflorens	Sweet-scented shrub, Monthly flowering	75
40 Calycanthus viridiflorus	Sweet-scented shrub, Green flowering	1 00
41 Calycanthus macrophyllus	Sweet-scented shrub, Californian large, twice blooming	50
42 **Caragana** arborescens	Siberian Pea tree	50
43 Caragana chamlagu	Caragana, Chinese	50
44 Caragana grandiflora	Caragana, Great Flowered	50
45 **Ceanothus** Americanus	New Jersey tea	25
46 **Cephalanthus** occidentalis	White Globe flower	25
47 **Ceratonia** siliqua	Carob tree	75
48 **Cercis** japonica	Judas tree, Japan, splendid	2 00
49 Cercis variegata	Judas tree, variegated-leaved	2 00
50 **Chimonanthus** fragrans	Japan Alspice	50 to 1 00
50½ **Clerodendron** Bungeana	Clerodendron, Chinese, beautiful, new	1 00
51 Clerodendron Kempferii	Clerodendron, Japan, beautiful, new	1 00
51½ **Clethra** alnifolia	Clethra, Fragrant	25
52 Clethra acuminata	Clethra, Acuminate-leaved	25
53 **Colutea** arborescens	Bladder Senna, Yellow	20
56 Colutea Alepica	Bladder Senna, Aleppo orange	25
57 Colutea cruenta vel orientalis	Bladder Senna, Oriental Red	38
58 **Corchorus**, see Kerria		
59 **Coriaria** myrtifolia	Coriaria, Myrtle leaved, beautiful foliage	25
60 **Cornus** sanguinea	Dogwood, Red twig	20
61 Cornus stricta, variegata	Dogwood, Silver-striped	50
62 Cornus mascula	Cornelian Cherry, Scarlet	50
63 Cornus fructu lutea	Cornelian Cherry, Golden	50
63½ Cornus mascula variegata	Cornelian Cherry, variegated	75
64 **Coronilla** emerus	Scorpion Senna	25
65 **Cotoneaster** acuminata	Cotoneaster, Acuminate	50
66 Cotoneaster affinis	Cotoneaster, Affinite	50
67 Cotoneaster rotundifolia	Cotoneaster, Round-leaved	50
68 **Crataegus** oxyacantha	Hawthorn, English	25 to 50
69 Crataegus, alba pleno	Hawthorn, Double white	50 to 75
70 Crataegus, rubra pleno	Hawthorn, Double crimson	75
71 Crataegus, monogyna rosea	Hawthorn, Pink	50 to 75
72 Crataegus, punicea	Hawthorn, Crimson	50 to 75
73 Crataegus, variegata	Hawthorn, Variegated-leaved	75

N. B.—Also, 10 other species which are but little ornamental.

Botanical Name.	Common Name.	Price.
74 **Cydonia** (Pyrus) Japonica	**Quince,** Japan scarlet flowering	25 to 50
75 Cydonia *alba*	Quince, Japan white or blush	50
76 Cydonia *umbicillata rosea*	Quince, Japan roseate, many fruit	1 00
77 Cydonia *atrosanguinea*	Quince, Japan crimson	1 00
78 Cydonia *aurantiaca*	Quince, Japan orange	1 50
81 Cydonia *rubra pleno*	Quince, Japan Double scarlet	1 00
82 Cydonia Maillardii	Quince, Maillardii	1 00
83 **Cyrilla** racemiflora	**Cyrilla,** Racemed	75
84 **Cytisus** capitatus	**Cytisus,** Cluster flower	25
85 Cytisus sessilifolius	Cytisus, Sessile-leaved	30
86 Cytisus scoparius	**Scotch Broom**	25
	Ditto, large size	50
87 **Daphne** mezereum	**Mezereon,** Pink	50
87½ Daphne album	Mezereon, White	50
88 **Deutzia** corymbosa	**Deutzia,** Corymbose	50
88½ Deutzia Californica	Deutzia, Californian	1 00
89 Deutzia canescens	Deutzia, Hoary-leaved	60
89½ Deutzia crenata	Deutzia, Crenate-leaved	25 to 50
90 Deutzia virgata	Deutzia, Twiggy	50
90½ Deutzia gracilis	Deutzia, Graceful, neat	25 to 50
91 Deutzia scabra	Deutzia, Scabrous, beautiful	25
92 Deutzia staminea	Deutzia, Large stamened	25 to 50
93 Deutzia undulata	Deutzia, Waved-leaved	50
94 **Diervilla** lutea	**Honeysuckle,** Acadian	30
95 **Dirca** palustris	**Leatherwood**	50
96 **Edgworthia** chrysantha	**Edgworthia**	1 00
98 **Eleagnus** Japonicus	Japan Oleaster	50
99 **Euonymus** Americanus	**Strawberry Tree,** American Red	25 to 38
100 Euonymus atropurpureus	Strawberry Tree, Crimson fruited	38
101 Euonymus Europeus	Strawberry Tree, European Scarlet	38
102 Euonymus ardens	Strawberry Tree, Bright Scarlet	50
103 Euonymus fructu albo	Strawberry Tree, White fruited	50
104 Euonymus atrorubens	Strawberry Tree, Deep Red fruited	75
105 Euonymus pallidus	Strawberry Tree, Pink fruited	75
106 Euonymus purpureus	Strawberry Tree, Purple fruited	75
107 Euonymus nanus	Strawberry Tree, Dwarf, Red fruit	38
108 Euonymus angustifolius	Strawberry Tree, Narrow-leaved	50
109 Euonymus latifolus	Strawberry Tree, Broad-leaved, large fruit	25 to 50
110 Euonymus hamiltonius	Strawberry Tree, Deep crimson	1 00
110½ Euonymus linifolius	Flax-leaved	25 to 50
111 Euonymus obovatus	Strawberry Tree, Obovate-leaved	60
112 Euonymus sarmentosus	Strawberry Tree, Dwarf trailing	50
113 Euonymus verrucosus	Strawberry Tree, Warted barked	50
114 Euonymus pendula	Strawberry Tree, Weeping	1 00
115 **Fontanesia** phyllyreoides	**Fontanesia,** Syrian	50
116 **Forsythia** viridissima	Japan Golden Bell, or Trinket flower	25 to 38
116½ Forsythia suspensa	Forsythia, Drooping Yellow	1 00
117 **Fortunea** sinensis	**Fortunea,** Chinese	1 00
118 **Fothergilla** alnifolia	**Fothergilla,** Fragrant	38
121 **Genista** tinctoria	**Broom,** Dyer's	30
122 Genista *flore pleno*	Broom, Double Dyer's	50
123 **Gordonia** pubescens	**Franklinia**	1 00
124 **Halesia** tetraptera	**Silver Bell,** or Snowdrop Tree	40
125 Halesia grandiflora	Silver Bell, Great flowered	1 00
126 Halesia parviflora	Silver Bell, Small flowered	50
127 Halesia *rosea*	Silver Bell, Rose tinted	1 00
128 Halesia diptera	Silver Bell, Two winged	50
129 **Helianthemum** appeninum	**Helianthemum,** Appenine Dwarf	50
130 **Hibiscus** syriacus	**Althea frutex,** or *Rose of Sharon*	
131 Hibiscus *bicolor*	Althea frutex, Single White, crimson center	20
132 Hibiscus niveus	Althea frutex, Single, snow white, beautiful	38

NOTE.—The following are all double flowering, except No. 159.

133 Hibiscus *albo pleno*	Althea frutex, White	25 to 50
134 Hibiscus *niveo pleno*	Althea frutex, Snowy white	50
135 Hibiscus *rubro pleno*	Althea frutex, Red	25 to 50
136 Hibiscus ardens	Althea frutex, Bright red	38
137 Hibiscus rosea	Althea frutex, Roseate	50
138 Hibiscus *rubra compacta*	Althea frutex, Red Anemone	38

Botanical Name.	Common Name.	Price.
138½ Hibiscus violacea semiplena......Althea frutex, Semi-double Violet......		38
139 Hibiscus cœrulescens...............Althea frutex, Blue.................		38
140 Hibiscus cœruleo-compacta ....Althea frutex, Blue Anemone..........		50
141 Hibiscus bicolor...................Althea frutex, Pleasant-eyed..........		38
142 Hibiscus albo variey...............Althea frutex, White striped.........		38
143 Hibiscus rosea-varieg..............Althea frutex, Roseate striped........		50
144 Hibiscus speciosa..................Althea frutex, Carnation striped.......		50
145 Hibiscus rubra pallida.............Althea frutex, Pale red shaded........		50
146 Hibiscus rosea bicolor.............Althea frutex, Rose and red shaded.....		50
147 Hibiscus atrorubens................Althea frutex, Crimson shaded.........		75
148 Hibiscus albicans..................Althea frutex, Incarnate, early flowering.		75
149 Hibiscus incarnata.................Althea frutex, Blush shaded..........		50
150 Hibiscus cœruleo purpurea..........Althea frutex, Bluish purple..........		50
151 Hibiscus lilacina..................Althea frutex, Lilac.................		50
152 Hibiscus pœonæflora................Althea frutex, Red Pæony flowered......		75
153 Hibiscus elegantissima.............Althea frutex, White, Blush, and Crimson		50
154 Hibiscus fastuosa..................Althea frutex, Imperial red...........		75
155 Hibiscus tricolor..................Althea frutex, Vermilion Tricolor, beautifully mottled and striped, very unique		75
156 Hibiscus picta....................Althea frutex, Semi-double Painted Lady.	25 to	50
157 Hibiscus purpurea pallida..........Althea frutex, Semi-double light purple...		50
158 Hibiscus rubro fol. aureis.........Althea frutex, Double red, gold striped leaves..............................		75
158½ Hibiscus profusa..................Althea frutex, Profuse, Blush, purple center		75
159 Hibiscus folio variegato..........Althea frutex, Variegated-leaved single...		50

N.B.—The above, with only four exceptions, will withstand our northern Winters.

161 Hippophæ rhamnoides...............Sea Buckthorn................		38
162 Hydrangea arborescens.............Hydrangea, White, tall........		38
163 Hydrangea hortensis...............Hydrangea, Blue and Pink......		25
164 Hydrangea variegata...............Hydrangea, Striped leaved......		50
165 Hydrangea japonica................Hydrangea, Japan blue.........		30
166 Hydrangea pubescens...............Hydrangea, Pubescent.........		75
167 Hydrangea quercifolia.............Hydrangea, Oak-leaved white....		50
168 Hydrangea raduta..................Hydrangea, Ray-flowered white...		38
169 Hypericum Kalmianum...............St. John's wort, Kalm's.......		25
170 Ilex prinoides....................Deciduous Holly...............		75
171 Itea virginica...................Virginian Itea................		50
172 Indigofera decora.................Indigo, Brilliant.............		1,00
173 Indigofera dosua..................Indigo, Dosua.................		1 00
174 Jasminum fruticans................Jasmin, Large-leaved yellow..........		38
175 Jasminum humile...................Jasmin, Italian small-leaved..........		38
176 Kerria, or Cor. horus.............Corchorus, Yellow.............		20
177 Lagerstrœmia indica...............Crape Myrtle, Pink...........	40 to	75
177½ Lagerstrœmia reginæ..............Crape Myrtle, Red	40 to	75
178 Lagerstrœmia violacea.............Crape Myrtle, Violet..........		40
178½ Lagerstrœmia purpurea............Crape Myrtle, Purple..........		40
179 Lagerstrœmia corallina............Crape Myrtle, Splendid Coral..........		1 50
180 Ligustrum italicum................Privet, Italian, sub-evergreen..........		20
181 Ligustrum variegatum..............Privet, Striped-leaved........		38
182 Ligustrum japonicum...............Privet, Japan Laurel-leaved....		50
183 Lycium Carolinianum...............Lycium, Carolina.............		1 00
184 Lonicera..........................Twining, Honeysuckles. (See page 45).		
185 Magnolia gracilis.................Magnolia, Japan purple, twice flowering..		1 00
186 Magnolia obovata..................Magnolia, Chinese Purple and White, blooms twice..................		75
187 Magnolia Thompsoniana.............Magnolia, Thompson's large white.......	2 to 3	00

Pæonia arborea, see Tree Pæonies, under distinct head.

188 Pavia macrostachya................Chestnut, Dwarf white........		50
189 Pavia floripleno..................Chestnut, Double flowering Dwarf.......		2 00
190 Philadelphus coronarius...........Syringa, European fragrant....		25
191 Philadelphus multiplex............Syringa, Double flowered..........		25 to 50
192 Philadelphus Gordonianus..........Syringa, Gordon's Oregon..........		25 to 38
193 Philadelphus grandiflorus.........Syringa, Garland, large flowers........		25
194 Philadelphus Himalayensis.........Syringa, Himalaya.............		1 00
195 Philadelphus gracilis.............Syringa, Slender branched........		38
196 Philadelphus nana.................Syringa, Dwarf...............		25
197 Philadelphus nivalis..............Syringa, Snow flowered..........		50

Botanical Name.	Common Name.	Price.
198 Philadelphus Sartianianus	Syringa, Japan, new	50
199 Philadelphus thyrsiflorus	Syringa, Thyrse flowered	50
200 Philadelphus virgatus	Syringa, Branching	50
201 Philadelphus Zeyherii	Syringa, Zeyher's beautiful	50
202 Philadelphus inodorus	Syringa, Scentless	25
203 **Potentilla** fruticosa	**Cinquefoil,** Shrubby	20
204 Potentilla floribunda	Cinquefoil, Profuse flowered	50
205 **Prinos** verticillatus	**Winterberry,** Scarlet	25
206 Prunus nigra, pleno	**Sloe,** Double flowering	50
206½ Ptelia trifoliata	Hop Tree	25
Punica	Pomegranate, see page 25.	
Pyrus Japonica, see *Cydonia*		
209 **Rhamnus** catharticus	**Buckthorn,** Purging	20
210 Rhamnus Carolinus	Buckthorn, Carolina, beautiful	1 00
211 Rhamnus Californicus	Buckthorn, California, beautiful	1 00
212 **Ribes** albidum	**Currant,** Snowy flowered, beautiful	75
213 Ribes alpinum	Currant, Alpine scarlet fruited	50
214 Ribes Bridgesii	Currant, Bridge's	50
215 Ribes Gordonianum	Currant, Gordon's orange and scarlet	50
216 Ribes setosum	Currant, Setose	
217 Ribes subvestitum	Currant, Californian, beautiful	1 00
218 Ribes cynosbati	Currant, Red prickly fruited	50
218½ Ribes malvaceum	Currant, Mallow-flowered	50
219 Ribes sanguineum	Currant, Scarlet flowering	50
220 Ribes, *flore pleno*	Currant, Double flowering	1 00
221 Ribes speciosum	Currant, Fuchsia flowered	50
222 Ribes tenuifolium	Currant, Yellow fruited	50
222½ Ribes Utah	Currant, Mormon	1 00
223 Ribes splendens	Currant, splendid	75

N. B.—For other Species, see pages 27 and 28.

223½ **Robinia** hispida	**Acacia,** Rose	25
224 Robinia macrophylla	Acacia, Weeping rose	50
225 **Rubus** cuneifolius	**Bramble,** Cuneiform	50
226 Rubus nobilis	Bramble, Noble purple	50
227 Rubus nootkanus	**Raspberry,** Snowy	50
228 Rubus odoratus	Raspberry, Purple flowered	16
229 Rubus rosæfolius	Raspberry, Chinese Dwarf Double white	38
230 Rubus spectabilis	Raspberry, Showy Purple	50

N. B.—For other Species, see Vines and Creepers.

231 **Salix,** see Osiers	**Willow,** see Osiers.	
232 **Sambucus,** *flore pleno*	**Elder,** Double flowering	50
233 Shepherdia argentea	Shepherdia, Silvery	50 to 75
Spartium, see *Cytisus* and *Genista*.		
235 **Spiraea** adiantoides	**Spiraea,** Adiantum-leaved dwarf	50
236 Spiraea alpina	Spiraea, Alpine	25 to 38
237 Spiraea amœna	Spiraea, Select cluster, white	50
238 Spiraea ariæfolia, vel sinensis	Spiraea, Aria-leaved white	50
239 Spiraea argentea	Spiraea, Silvery-leaved	25 to 38
240 Spiraea bella	Spiraea, Chinese dwarf, pink	25 to 35
241 Spiraea betulæfolia	Spiraea, Birch-leaved	25
242 Spiraea Billardieri	Spiraea, Billard's bright rosy	1 00
243 Spiraea Blumei	Spiraea, Blume's bright pink	1 00
243½ Spiraea Californica	Spiraea, Californian white	50
244 Spiraea callosa vel Fortunei	Spiraea, Chinese pink panicled	30 to 50
245 Spiraea candicans	Spiraea, Hoary	50
246 Spiraea chamœdrifolia	Spiraea, White Germander	25
247 Spiraea corymbosa	Spiraea, Corymbose white	20
248 Spiraea crenata	Spiraea, White crenate-leaved	25
248½ Spiraea cretica	Spiraea, Cretan	25
249 Spiraea Daurica	Spiraea, Daurian	50
250 Spiraea Douglassii	Spiraea, Douglass' fine red monthly	25 to 38
251 Spiraea eximia	Spiraea, California pink, beautiful, monthly	75
252 Spiraea flexuosa	Spiraea, Flexile	50
253 Spiraea floribunda	Spiraea, Profuse-flowered	50
254 Spiraea grandiflora alba	Spiraea, Chinese large white	75
255 Spiraea grandiflora rosea	Spiraea, Large rose-colored	50

5

Botanical Name.	Common Name.	Price.
256 Spiræa Hookerii	Spiræa, Hooker's new	1 00
257 Spiræa hypericifolia	Spiræa, Hypericum-leaved	25
258 Spiræa lævigata	Spiræa, Siberian dwarf white	50
259 Spiræa Lindleyana	Spiræa, Lindley's white	25
260 Spiræa nepalensis	Spiræa, Nepal white	25
261 Spiræa nikandertii	Spiræa, Nikandert's Silver Wreath	50
261½ Spiræa nivea	Spiræa, Snowy	50
262 Spiræa oblongifolia	Spiræa, Long-leaved	50
263 Spiræa opulifolia	Spiræa, Guelder Rose	25
264 Spiræa, fol. lutea	Spiræa, Guelder Rose, yellow leaves	50
265 Spiræa ovata	Spiræa, Oval leaved white	50
266 Spiræa paniculata alba	Spiræa, White, panicled	25
267 Spiræa paniculata rosea	Spiræa, Rose-panicled	25
268 Spiræa prunifolia pleno	Spiræa, Japan double white	25 to 38
269 Spiræa Reevesiana	Spiræa, Reeve's Chinese white, beautiful	25 to 38
270 Spiræa Reevesiana pleno	Spiræa, Reeve's Chinese double white	50
271 Spiræa rotundifolia	Spiræa, Round-leaved	38
271½ Spiræa rupestris	Spiræa, Rupestris	75
272 Spiræa salicifolia alba	Spiræa, Willow-leaved white	20
273 Spiræa salicifolia rosea	Spiræa, Willow-leaved, deep pink, dense spike	25
274 Spiræa salicifolia incarnata	Spiræa, Blush pink	25
275 Spiræa sinensis pendula	Spiræa, Chinese pendulous red	50
276 Spiræa sorbifolia	Spiræa, Sorb-leaved cluster	25
277 Spiræa sinensis albo	Spiræa, Chinese white cluster	50
278 Spiræa thalictroides	Spiræa, Thalictrum-leaved white	50
279 Spiræa tomentosa	Spiræa, Downy red-spiked	20
280 Spiræa trilobata	Spiræa, Three-lobe leaved	50
281 Spiræa ulmifolia	Spiræa, Elm leaved white	20
282 Spiræa vaccinifolia	Spiræa, Vaccinium-leaved	50

N. B.—The Spiræas are exceedingly neat, and profuse flowering Shrubs, of easy culture, and very hardy.

283 Staphylea trifolia	Bladdernut, Trinket flower	38
284 Staphylea pinnata	Bladdernut, Pinnated	50
285 Stuartia malacodendron	Stewartia, Virginian	1 00
286 Stuartia pentagynia	Stewartia, Maryland	75
287 Styrax officinale	Storax, Officinal, *beautiful flowers*	50
288 Styrax lævigatum	Storax, Dwarf white	50
289 Symphoria racemosa	Snowberry	18
290 Symphoria glauca	Snowberry, Dwarf	50
291 Symphoria glomerata	Indian Currant	18
292 Symphoria variegata	Indian Currant, Variegated	25
Syringa	Lilac.	
294 Syringa vulgaris *cerulea*	Lilac, Purple or Blue	20
295 Syringa *purpurea plena*	Lilac, Double purple	1 00
296 Syringa *rubra*	Lilac, Marly Hybrid, or Purple	25
297 Syringa *alba*	Lilac, Large white	20 to 50
298 Syringa *alba plena*	Lilac, Double white	1 00
299 Syringa *variegata*	Lilac, Variegated-leaved	1 00
300 Syringa *bicolor*	Lilac, Bicolor	1 00
301 Syringa *regalis*	Lilac, Royal purple	50
302 Syringa *Caroli X*	Lilac, Charles X., fine large purple	40
303 Syringa *grandiflora*	Lilac, Large purple	40
304 Syringa *Persica*	Lilac, Persian purple	25 to 38
305 Syringa *alba-cerulea vel bicolor*	Lilac, Persian blush white, or Bicolor	35 to 50
306 Syringa *nivea*	Lilac, Persian snow-white	75
307 Syringa *lacciniata*	Lilac, Persian cut-leaved	25 to 50
308 Syringa *chinensis*	Lilac, Chinese bluish purple	25 to 50
309 Syringa *rothonagensis, vel Sanguinea rubra*	Lilac, Siberian red	50
310 Syringa *rothonagensis alba*	Lilac, Hybrid white	1 00
311 Syringa sinensis alba	Lilac, Chinese new white	1 00
312 Syringa Josikea	Lilac, Chionanthus-leaved	50
313 Syringa Emodii	Lilac, Nepal	50 to 1 00
314 Syringa Delepine	Lilac, Delepine	1 00
315 Syringa Valletteana	Lilac, Vallettiana	50
316 Tamarix gallica	Tamarisk, French	25
317 Tamarix germanica	Tamarisk, German	25

SELECTIONS OF FLOWERING SHRUBS.

Most persons are so well acquainted with these, that we will only remark to those least acquainted, that, for general ornament, amateurs usually select the different varieties of Double Althea, Azalea, Calycanthus, Deutzia, Hawthorn, Japan Quince, Euonymus, Forsythia, Groundsel-tree, Magnolia, Clethra, Philadelphus, Rose Acacia, Spiraea, Lilac, Upright Honeysuckle, Weigela, Tamarisk, Viburnum, Flowering currant, Hydrangea, Syringa, &c.

OSIER—BASKET WILLOW.

Plants $2 per dozen, and $12 per 100. Scions $1 per 100, and $4 to $5 per 1000; and Salix viminalis in quantities of 25,000 or more, $2½ to $3 per 1000. No less than $1 worth will be supplied of any kind. N. B.—Directions for culture therewith.

1 Acutifolia, for dry soil.
2 Alba, Bedford, or Fence Willow.
3 Alba femina.
4 Alba mascula.
5 Annularis.
6 Argentea.
7 Babylonica nigra.
8 Beveridge, for hedge, a synonym.
9 Bicolor.
10 Caprea, for dry soil.
11 Caprea variegated, for dry soil.
12 Comewell.
13 Daphnoides.
14 Decipiens.
15 Forbyana, for fine basket work.
16 Gloucestershire, or Tockington.
17 Helix Viminalis of Colby, long clean shoots, superior.
18 Helix femina.
19 Holosericea.
20 Laurifolia.
21 Longskin, a synonym.
22 Mollissima (London).
23 Nigra.
24 Pentandria.
25 Purpurea, see Rubra.
26 Rosmarinifolia, or Pack-thread willow, long slender shoots, purple bark.
27 Rubra, or Purpurea, most esteemed by Coopers and Basket-makers.
28 Rubra, or Purpurea mascula.
29 Russelliana.
30 Starkianum.
31 Stipularis.
32 Triandra femina, longest leaves.
33 Triandra mascula, bright golden clean shoots for fine basket work.
34 Viminalis femina, clean bark, greenish yellow in winter.
35 Viminalis mascula.
36 Violacea.
37 Viridis.
38 Vitellina, or Aurea.

UPRIGHT HONEYSUCKLES.

Botanical Name.	Common Name.	Price.
38½ Xylosteum caucasicum,	Oriental, or Caucasian white	50
39 Xylosteum cœruleum	Blue-berried	35
40 Xylosteum ciliatum	Ciliated-leaved	50
41 Xylosteum Ledebourii	Californian yellow and red, evergreen	25 to 35
42 Xylosteum occidentale	Occidental	50
43 Xylosteum Sibericum luteum	Siberian yellow, very beautiful	75
44 Xylosteum Thomasii	Thomas' new	1 00
45 Xylosteum tartaricum	Tartarian, early red	20 to 30
46 Xylosteum *albiflora*	Tartarian early white	20 to 35
47 Xylosteum *grandiflora*	Tartarian bright red, variegated, splendid	50
48 Xylosteum officinale	European straw-colored	20 to 35
49 Xylosteum solonis	American yellow	50

TWINING HONEYSUCKLES.

Lonicera	Honeysuckle.	
51 Caprifolium rubrum	Early blush or Red Italian	35
52 Caprifolium album	Early white Italian	50
53 Caprifolium sempervirens	Italian Evergreen	50
54 **Periclymenum**	English Woodbine	20 to 38
55 Belgicum	Striped monthly	20 to 35
56 Flavum	Yellowish Woodbine	50
57 Serotinum	Late red cluster	50
58 Periclymenum Quercifolium	Oak-leaved white	50
59 Variegatum	Variegated oak-leaved	50
60 Glauca	Glaucous-leaved	75
61 Canadensis	Canada straw-colored	30
62 Canescens	Algiers hoary-leaved white	50
62½ Ciliata	Californian Ciliated	1 00
63 Confusa vel Japonica	Japan straw-colored	25 to 38
64 Etrusca	Etruscan, or Tuscany	50
65 Douglassii, *blooms in June*	Douglass' straw-colored, ovate-leaved	50
66 Sempervirens	Scarlet trumpet monthly	35
67 Sempervirens minor vel grata	Small deep scarlet trumpet, or Evergreen monthly	50
68 Brownii	Superb bright scarlet	35
69 Bicolor superba	Scarlet and yellow monthly	75
70 **Flava**, vel Fraseri	Yellow trumpet monthly	35
70½ Macrophyllum, round glaucous leaves	Large perfoliate-leaved, straw colored	50
71 Occidentalis	Oregon orange-colored, twice flowering	1 00
72 Parviflora	Small dark yellow	30
73 Pubescens	Pubescent orange-colored	35
74 Flexnosa vel sinensis	Chinese Evergreen monthly, fragrant	20 to 35
75 Japonica, Villossissima alba	Japan Evergreen, pure white flowers	50
76 Brachypoda	Brachypoda	30 to 50
77 Fragrantissima	Chinese Fragrant, new	1 00
78 Implexa	Minorca purplish	50
80 Magnevillei	Magneville's Chinese white, blooms April	50
81 Romana	Roman	50
82 Speciosissima	Specious, or Showy	50
83 Splendida vel splendens	Brilliant scarlet	30 to 50
84 Sulphurea	Sulphur-colored	30
85 Standishii	Standish's Fragrant	30
86 Vaccinifolia	Vaccinium-leaved	50
87 Villossissima	Velvet Tuscan, white	38
88 Fortunei	Fortune's Chinese	1 00
89 Spectabilis	Chinese splendid	75

N. B.—Extra Large plants of several of the best varieties at 50 to 75 cents.

VINES AND CREEPERS.

87½ **Ampelopsis** hederacea	Virginia **Creeper**	20
88½ Ampelopsis bipinnata	Bipinnate-leaved Creeper, delicate foliage	50
89½ Ampelopsis Roylei	Royle's Creeper	75
90 Ampelopsis cordata	Cordate-leaved Creeper	38
91 Ampelopsis tricolor. *Vitis variegata.*	Tricolor-leaved, beautiful	30 to 50
92 **Apios** (Glycine) tuberosa	Purple Cluster Glycine (Herbaceous)	25
93 **Aristolochia** sipho	Dutchman's Pipe vine	38 to 50

VINES AND CREEPERS. 45

Botanical Name.	Common Name.	Price.
94 Aristolochia tomentosa (pubescens)	Downy-leaved Pipe vine	50
95 Aristolochia altissima	Lofty-growing Pipe vine	50
96 Aristolochia Kempferii	Kempfer's Pipe vine	75
97 Aristolochia serpentaria	Medicinal Pipe vine (Herbaceous)	25
98 **Asclepias nigra**	**Swallowwort,** Black-flowered (Herbaceous)	38
99 **Atragene alpina**	**Atragene,** Alpine pale blue	1 00
100 Atragene americana	Atragene, American deep blue	50
101 Atragene sibirica	Atragene, Siberian white	1 00
102 **Berchemia** vel zizyphus volubilis	**Berchemia,** Twining, beautiful	1 00
103 **Bignonia radicans**	**Trumpet-flower,** Scarlet	20
104 Bignonia *coccinea vel prœcox*	Trumpet-flower, Red	30
105 Bignonia flava speciosa	Trumpet-flower, Golden or Superb scarlet	50
106 Bignonia grandiflora	Trumpet-flower, Chinese large orange-colored	25 to 50
107 Bignonia *atrosanguinea vel purpurea*	Trumpet-flower, Chinese deep crimson	50
108 Bignonia *aurantia*	Prince's Orange, colored hybrid	75
109 Bignonia *Princei*	Trumpet-flower, Prince's deep scarlet Hybrid	75
110 Bignonia alba	Trumpet-flower, White-flowering	75
Bignonia capreolata, see Evergreen Climbers.		
112 **Brachybotria rosea**	Glycine, Pale violet	1 00
113 **Celastrus scandens**	**Bittersweet,** American	20
114 Celastrus edulis	Bittersweet, Edible-fruited	75
115 **Calystegia pubescens**	**Convolvulus,** Rose and white striped	50
116 Calystegia pubescens pleno	Convolvulus, Double Pink	20
117 **Clematis** azurea grandiflora	**Virgin's Bower,** Japan large blue	50
118 Clematis campaniflora	Virgin's Bower, White bell-flowered	50
119 Clematis crispa	Virgin's Bower, Curled Bell	30
120 Clematis flammula	Virgin's Bower, White Vanilla-scented	25 to 50
121 Clematis florida vel Indica	Virgin's Bower, Japan White	50
121½ Clematis florida vel Indica plena	Virgin's Bower, Japan double White	50
122 Clematis Louise (Japan)	Virgin's Bower, Louise	50
123 Clematis Amelia (Japan)	Virgin's Bower, Amelia	50
124 Clematis *Grahamii*	Virgin's Bower, Graham's Japan	1 00
125 Clematis *Helena*	Virgin's Bower, Helena	50
126 Clematis *Monstrosa*	Virgin's Bower, Monstrosa	50
127 Clematis Sophia	Virgin's Bower, Sophia	50
128 Clematis Hartwegi, vel Anemœflora, vel montana	Virgin's Bower, Californian large white, blooms in May	40
129 Clematis Cylindrica	Virgin's Bower, Cylindric Blue	50
130 Clematis Hendersoni	Virgin's Bower, Henderson's large Blue	75
131 Clematis cœrulea odorata	Virgin's Bower, Blue Vanilla-scented, monthly	1 00
133 Clematis Nepalensis	Virgin's Bower, Nepal autumn-flowered	75
134 Clematis Orientalis	Virgin's Bower, Oriental yellow	50
135 Clematis Orientalis cœrulea	Virgin's Bower, Oriental pale blue	50
136 Clematis Pallasii	Virgin's Bower, Pallas'	1 00
138 Clematis Sieboltii bicolor	Virgin's Bower, Japan bicolor	50
139 Clematis smilacifolia	Virgin's Bower, Smilax large-leaved	50
140 Clematis viorna	Virgin's Bower, Reflexed red	25
141 Clematis Virginiana	Virgin's Bower, Virginian white	20
142 Clematis vitalba	Virgin's Bower, Traveler's Joy	38
143 Clematis Alpina	Virgin's Bower, Alpine pale blue	35
144 Clematis lanuginosa	Virgin's Bower, Woolly	74
145 Clematis revoluta	Virgin's Bower, Revolute petaled	50
146 Clematis viticella	Virgin's Bower, Purple	25 to 50
147 Clematis *atrorubens*	Virgin's Bower, Dark red	50
148 Clematis cœrulea	Virgin's Bower, Blue	25
149 Clematis *purpurea plena*	Virgin's Bower, Double purple	50
150 Clematis *pulchella*	Virgin's Bower, Bright pink	50
151 Clematis *rubra*	Virgin's Bower, Red flowered	30
The three following species are not Climbers.		
152 Clematis erecta	Alpine Upright White	25
153 Clematis integrifolia	Hungarian Upright Blue	25
154 Clematis Mongolica tubulosa	Mongolian Bright Azure	75
155 **Cocculus** Carolinus	Carolinian Cocculus	75
Cynancham. (See Gonolobium.)		
156 **Dioscorea** villosa	Wild Yam, American (Herbaceous)	50

Botanical Name.	Common Name.	Price.
157 Dioscorea batatas................	Chinese Potato, exquisite odor.........	50
158 Echites difformis.................	Echites, Twining...................	50
159 **Convolvulus panduratus**...........	**Convolvulus**, Large white (Herbaceous)...	38
160 Convolvulus *flore pleno*..........	Convolvulus, Double white do	75
161 Convolvulus europeus albus.........	Convolvulus, European white do	38
162 Convolvulus repens................	Convolvulus, Trailing small white (Herbaceous)...................	25
163 Convolvulus Dahurica..............	Convolvulus, Dahurian (Herbaceous).....	50
Forsythia. (See Shrubs.)		
Glycine. (See Wistaria.)		
166 Gonolobium læve..................	Twining Gonolobium (Herbaceous)......	88
Hedera. (See Evergreen Climbers)....Ivy. (See Evergreen Climbers.)		
168 Humulus lupulus..................	Hop vine......................	20
170 Jasminum Officinale..............	Jasmine, White flowering Officinal......	20 to 35
171 Chrysophyllum....................	Jasmine, Striped-leaved white..........	50
172 Ochroleucum.....................	Jasmine, Large Yellow..............	35
For others, see Evergreen Climbers.		
173 Kadsura Japonica.................	Kadsura, Japan yellow..............	50
Lonicera. see page 44...............	Honeysuckle, see page 44.	
176 Lycium barbarum.................	Box Thorn, or Blue Jasmine.........	20
177 Lycium europeum................	Box Thorn, European scarlet-berried....	50
178 Mandevillea suaveolens...........	Mandevillea, Fragrant...............	50
179 Menispermum canadense..........	Moonseed, Canadian................	38 to 50
180 Menispermum Dauricum..........	Moonseed, Daurian................	75
181 Passiflora incarnata..............	Passion flower, Hardy blush..........	38
182 Passiflora incarnata alba..........	Passion flower, White flowered........	50
183 Passiflora palmata...............	Passion flower, Purple palmate........	50
184 Passiflora cerulea...............	Passion flower, Blue flowered.........	35
185 Passiflora Shropeana.............	Passion flower, Shropean............	50
For other species, see Green-House Catalogue.		
186 Periploca græca.................	Grecian silk vine..................	20 to 38
	Ditto, large size....................	50
Rosa............................	Roses, Climbing varieties, see Rose Catalogue.	
Rubus...........................	Flowering Bramble. See Evergreen Climbers.	
Rubus...........................	Flowering Raspberry. See page 41.	
190 Schisandra lutea................	Schisandra, Japan yellow............	1 00
191 Schisandra coccinea.............	Schisandra, Scarlet................	75
192 Smilax tamnoides...............	Smilax, Carolina.................	38
193 Smilax peduncularis............	Smilax, Peduncled................	38
Vinca, see Evergreen Climbers.		
195 Vitis odoratissima...............	Grape, Mignonette scented...........	50
For other Grapes, see Special Catalogue of Grapes.		
197 Wistaria frutescens (Glycine)......	Wistaria, American purple...........	20 to 35
198 Wistaria frutescens nivea..........	Wistaria, American Snow-white, twice flowering....................	1 50
199 Wistaria magnifica..............	Wistaria, Magnificent American........	1 00
200 Wistaria floribunda vel purpurascens..	Wistaria, Large spiked cerulean, beautiful, blooms twice, most vigorous........	1 00
201 Wistaria sinensis...............	Wistaria, Chinese large blue, blooms twice....................	35 to 50
	Ditto, largest size..................	1 00
202 Wistaria sinensis alba............	Wistaria, Chinese large white..........	1 00
203 Wistaria brachypoda.............	Wistaria, Brachypoda...............	1 00
204 Wistaria violacea...............	Wistaria, Violet colored, blooms twice...	1 00
205 Wistaria brachybotris rosea........	Wistaria, Pale violet, blooms twice......	1 00

EVERGREEN CLIMBERS.

208 Akebia quinata..................	Akebia, Chinese, shining leaves, neat flowers.....................	50
209 **Aristolochia** sempervirens........	**Birthwort**, Evergreen.............	50
210 Aristolochia Kempferi............	Birthwort, Kempfer's..............	75
211 **Bignonia** crucigera (capreolata).....	Orange-colored Trumpetflower.......	35 to 50
212 **Clematis** sempervirens...........	Fragrant white Clematis............	50
213 **Decumaria** sarmentosa...........	Climbing Decumaria..............	25 to 50
214 **Dioclea** glycinoides.............	Scarlet Dioclea, (like Glycine)........	1 00
214½ Gelseminum nitidum.............	Jasmine, Carolina yellow............	25 to 38

	Botanical Name.	Common Name.	Price.
215	**Hedera** helix	Ivy, European Evergreen	20
216	Hedera variegata argentea	Ivy, Variegated leaved	50
217	Hedera hibernica vel Canariensis	Ivy, Irish, large foliage	25 to 35
218	Hedera hibernica striata	Ivy, Striped leaved Irish	50
219	Hedera arborescens	Ivy, Tree or shrubby	50
220	Hedera Algeriensis	Ivy, Algiers	50
221	Hedera Caucasica	Ivy, Caucasian	50
222	Hedera Ragueniana	Ivy, Large heart leaved	30 to 50
223	Hedera Chrysocarpa vel Poetica	Ivy, Classic or Poetic yellow berried	50
224	Hedera palmata vel digitata	Ivy, Palmate-leaved	35 to 50
225	Hedera Ponderata	Ivy, Ponderous	50
225½	Hedera latifolia	Ivy, Broad leaved	50
226	**Jasminum** fruticans	Jasmine, Broad-leaved yellow	25 to 35
227	Jasminum pubigerum (Wallichianum)	Jasmine, Nepal yellow	25 to 50
227½	Jasminum humile	Jasmin, Italian small leaved	35
228	Jasminum nudiflorum	Jasmine, Early yellow	35 to 50
228½	Jasminum Reevesii	Jasmine, Reeves' Chinese	75
229	Jasminum tenuifolium	Jasmine, Narrow-leaved	75
229½	Jasminum revolutum (triumphans)	Jasmine, Revolute, large yellow	25 to 35
230	Jasminum Fortunei	Jasmine, Fortune's Chinese	50
231	Jasminum Poiteau	Jasmine, Poiteau	50
	For other Jasmonines, see preceding page.		
232	**Lonicera** flexuosa	**Honeysuckle,** Chinese fragrant, monthly	25 to 35
233	Lonicera Japonica Villossissima alba	Honeysuckle, Japan white	50
	Rosa	**Roses,** *Climbing varieties,* see Rose Catalogue.	
235	**Rubus** lacciniatus	Parsley-leaved Blackberry	50
236	Rubus inermis	Bramble, Thornless	50
237	Rubus fruticosus plena	Bramble, Double white, resembling small roses	38
238	Rubus bellediflorus plena	Bramble, Double pink daisy-flowered, beautiful	50
239	**Ruscus** racemosus	Classic Laurel, beautiful foliage	1 00
240	**Ryncospermum** Jasminoides	Jasmine-leaved Ryncospermum	50
241	**Smilax** tamnoides	**Smilax,** Carolina	50
242	**Stauntonia** latifolia	**Stauntonia,** Broad-leaved, rapid growth	50 to 75
242½	Stauntonia amabilis	Stauntonia, Lovely	50 to 75
243	Stauntonia toluccensis	Stauntonia, Tolucca	75
244	**Vinca** minor	**Periwinkle,** or Running Myrtle, Blue	25
244½	Vinca bicolor	Periwinkle, white and blue flowers distinct	38
245	Vinca cærulea plena	Periwinkle, Double blue	50
246	Vinca albiflora	Periwinkle, White-flowered	25
247	Vinca punicea	Periwinkle, Purple-flowering	38
248	Vinca punicea plena	Periwinkle, Double red or purple	50
249	Vinca cærulea variegata	Periwinkle, Gold-striped, blue flowers	25
250	Vinca variegata, alba	Periwinkle, Gold-striped, white flowers	50
251	Vinca major	Periwinkle, Broad-leaved, large flowers	38

N. B.—The Vincas are very suitable for Cemeteries, and will be supplied at $25 per 1,000.

———— •✦• ————

EVERGREEN TREES.—CONIFERÆ.

Including the new and rare species recently introduced. Amateurs of the favorite family of Evergreen Trees, will not fail to notice the great superiority of this collection over any other offered for sale, and especially when fine Evergreens are so scarce and desirable. Extra large Spruces and Pines, and many other species, can be supplied at proportionate prices. Small Seedling trees, of 1, 2, and 3 years, being of much less value, will be supplied at very moderate rates. The different Catalogue prices for Evergreen Trees, form no criterion, as their value depends upon the age and size.

	Botanical Name.	Common Name.	Price.
1	**Abies** Alba	**Spruce,** White American	75
	Do., 4 to 10 feet, at proportionate rates.		
2	Abies Argentea	Spruce, White European, very beautiful	1 00
	Do., 4 to 8 feet, at proportionate rates.		
3	Abies acutissima	Spruce, Acute-leaved	2 00
4	Abies amabilis	Spruce, Californian beautiful	2 00
5	Abies Brunoniana	Spruce, Alpine silvery Dwarf	2 to 3 00

Botanical Name.	Common Name.	Price.
6 Abies Canadensis	Spruce, Hemlock or Weeping	75
Do., 4 to 8 feet, at proportionate rates.		
Abies Cephalonica. *See Picea.*		
8 Abies Cerulea	Spruce, Bluish European, beautiful	1 to 2 00
9 Abies Clanbrasilliana	Spruce, Clanbrasill's dwarf	1 00
9½ Abies conica	Spruce, Conical	1 00
10 Abies Douglasii	Spruce, Douglass' Californian	2 to 3 00
11 Abies diffusa	Spruce, Diffuse	2 00
12 Abies Excelsa	Spruce, Norway, according to size	50 to 1 00
Do., 6 to 15 feet at proportionate prices.		
13 Abies Gregorii	Spruce, Gregory's Dwarf	2 00
14 Abies Menziesii	Spruce, Menzies' Oregon	1 50 to 2 00
15 Abies Morinda (*Smithiana*)	Spruce, Himalaya (1 to 6 ft., $1 per foot)	1 00
16 Abies Nigra	Spruce, Black or double	50
17 Abies Novæ Hollandiæ	Spruce, New Holland	2 00
17½ Abies orientalis	Spruce, Oriental	1 00
18 Abies orientalis vera	Spruce, Oriental	2 to 3 00
19 Abies pyramidalis	Spruce, Pyramidal	2 00
20 Abies pygmæa	Spruce, Liliputian	2 00
21 Abies Pinsapo. *See Picea.*		
22 Abies rubra	Spruce, Red or Double	50
23 Abies spectabilis. *See Picea.*		
24 **Araucaria** Imbricata	Chili Pine	2 00
25 Araucaria Lanceolata	Chinese lance-leaved pine	2 to 5 00
26 Araucaria Braziliensis	Brazil pine	2 50 to 5 00
27 Araucaria Bidwilli	Bidwill's pine	3 to 5 00
28 Araucaria Gracilis vel elegans	Graceful pine	5 to 8 00

N. B.—The last four require protection north of Charleston.

29 **Biota.** See Thuya.		
30 **Cedrus** Africanus viridis	Cedar, African green, beautiful, most hardy, rapid growth	2 00
Do., extra size, 3 to 12 feet, $1 per foot.		
31 Cedrus Deodara	Cedar, Deodar Silvery foliage	50 to 2 00
Do., extra size, 3 to 8 ft. 75 cts. per foot.		
32 Cedrus Deodara robusta	Cedar, Robust Deodar	1 00
33 Cedrus Libani	Cedar of Lebanon	2 00
Do., extra size, 3 to 8 ft., $1 per foot.		
34 Cedrus Libani argentea	Mount Atlas Silvery Cedar	2 00
Do., 3 to 12 feet, $1 per foot.		
35 **Cephalotaxus** Drupacea	Drupe-bearing Yew	1 50
36 Cephalotaxus Fortunei	Fortune's Chinese Yew	50 to 2 00
37 Cephalotaxus Montana	Mountain Yew	3 00
38 Cephalotaxus Pedunculata	Pedunculate Yew	2 00
39 Cephalotaxus Sinensis	Chinese Yew	1 00
40 Chamæcyparis nana	Chamæcyparis, Dwarf	1 00
41 Cerasus Caroliniana	Wild Orange (tender)	50 to 75
42 **Cryptomeria** Japonica	Japan Weeping Cypress	1 00
Do., 4 to 10 feet, at 75 cts. per foot.		
43 Cryptomeria Lobbiana	Japan dense-leaved Cypress	2 to 3 00
44 Cryptomeria Nana	Japan dwarf Cypress	1 00
45 **Cunninghamia** sinensis	Chinese lanceolate Cunninghamia	1 to 2 00
46 **Cupressus** Australis	Cypress, Australian	1 00
47 Cupressus Chinensis (pendula)	Cypress, Chinese pendulous	2 00
48 Cupressus Erecta	Cypress, Erect	1 50
49 Cupressus Ericoides	Cypress, Heath-leaved	1 00
50 Cupressus elegans	Cypress, elegant	1 00
51 Cupressus Flagelliformis	Cypress, Flagelliform	2 to 3 00
52 Cupressus Funebris	Cypress, Chinese funebral	50 to 1 50
53 Cupressus Gossanthanea	Cypress, Gossanthanea	2 00
54 Cupressus Goveniana	Cypress, Gowen's pale green	75 to 1 00
55 Cupressus Gracilis	Cypress, Graceful	3 00
56 Cupressus horizontalis	Cypress, Spreading	50 to 1 00
57 Cupressus Japonica	Cypress, Japan	2 00
58 Cupressus Knightiana elegans	Cypress Knight's	2 00
59 Cupressus Thuyæfolia	Cypress, Thuya-leaved	1 00
60 Cupressus Lawsoniana	Cypress, Lawson's Californian	2 00
61 Cupressus Lambertiana	Cypress, Lambert's	1 to 2 00
62 Cupressus Lusitanica glauca	Cypress, Portuguese glaucous	1 00

Botanical Name.	Common Name.	Price.
63 Cupressus Macrocarpa	Cypress, Large-coned,	1 to 1 50
64 Cupressus Mexicana	Cypress, Mexican pyramid, 2 to 4 feet	1 to 2 00
65 Cupressus McNabiana	Cypress, McNab's Californian	2 00
66 Cupressus montana	Cypress, Mountain	50
67 Cupressus Pyramidalis	Cypress, Pyramidal, beautiful	50 to 1 00
68 Cupressus Religiosa	Cypress, Sacred	2 00
69 Cupressus Reevesiana	Cypress, Reeve's Chinese	1 to 2 00
70 Cupressus stricta	Cypress, Upright	50
71 Cupressus Thuyoides	American white cedar	50
72 Cupressus Thuyoides variegata	Gold variegated cedar	2 to 3 00
73 Cupressus Torulosa	Cypress, Twisted Nepal	75
74 Cupressus Tournefortii	Cypress, Tournefort's	1 to 2 00
75 Cupressus Uhdeana	Cypress, Uhdeana	2 00
76 **Fitzroya Patagonica**	**Patagonian Fitzroy**	3 to 5 00
77 Ilex opaca	Holly American	75
78 **Juniperus Argentea**	**Juniper,** Silvery-leaved, beautiful	1 50

Do., 3 to 8 feet, $1 per foot.

79 Juniperus Bacciformis	Juniper, Berry-bearing	1 50
80 Juniperus Bedfordiana	Juniper, Bedford	50
81 Juniperus Bermudiana	Juniper, Bermudas Cedar	1 50
82 Juniperus Californica	Juniper, Californian	2 00
83 Juniperus Caroliniana	Juniper, Carolina Spiral	75 to 1 00
84 Juniperus Chinensis	Juniper, Chinese	40 to 75
85 Juniperus cinerascens	Juniper, Cinerascent	2 00
86 Juniperus Communis	Juniper, English	50
87 Juniperus Communis pendula	Juniper, Weeping English	75
88 Juniperus Cracovica	Juniper, Cracow dark green	35
89 Juniperus Dioica	Juniper, Diœcious	1 50
90 Juniperus Dumosa, vel decumbens	Juniper, Dense-leaved dwarf, beautiful	75
91 Juniperus Echinoformis	Juniper, Echinoform	75
92 Juniperus Ericoides	Juniper, Heath-like	50 to 1 00
93 Juniperus Excelsa	Juniper, Himalaya	75
94 Juniperus Flaccida	Juniper, Flaccid	1 25
95 Juniperus fragrans	Juniper, Fragrant	75
96 Juniperus Gossanthanea	Juniper, Gossanthanea	2 00
97 Juniperus Hermanii	Juniper, Herman's	2 00
98 Juniperus Hibernica	Juniper, Irish spiral, beautiful, exceedingly hardy	75

Do., 3 to 4 feet, 50 cents per foot. Do., 5 to 8 feet, 75 cts. per foot.

99 Juniperus Japonica	Juniper, Japan	2 00
100 Juniperus Langoldii	Juniper, Langold's	75
101 Juniperus Oblonga pendula	Juniper, Oblong Weeping	75 to 1 00
102 Juniperus Oxycedrus	Juniper, Brown-berried	1 50
103 Juniperus Phœnicea, or Lycia	Juniper, Phœnician	50 to 75
104 Juniperus Prostrata	Juniper, Trailing	40
105 Juniperus pyramidalis	Juniper, Pyramidal	75
106 Juniperus pyriformis	Juniper, Californian pyriform	1 25
107 Juniperus Recurva	Juniper, Recurved, or Pendulous	1 00
108 Juniperus Reevesiana (*Flagelliformis*)	Juniper, Reeve's Flagelliform	75
109 Juniperus Religiosa	Juniper, Sacred	1 75
110 Juniperus Sabina vera	European Savin	38 to 50
111 Juniperus Sabina variegata	Variegated Savin	75
111½ Juniperus Sphœrica	Juniper, Spherical	2 00
112 Juniperus Squamata	Juniper, Scaly	38 to 50
113 Juniperus Suecica	Juniper, Swedish Conical, beautiful, exceedingly hardy	35 to 75

Do., 3 to 4 feet, 50 cts. per foot. Do., 5 to 10 feet, 75 cts. per foot.

114 Juniperus Tamariscifolia	Juniper, Tamarisk-leaved Savin	50 to 75
115 Juniperus Thurifera	Juniper, Spanish Incense	60
116 Juniperus Virginiana	Red Cedar, (extra size 50 cts. to $1)	25
117 Juniperus Virginiana glauca	Red Cedar, Glaucous	60
118 Juniperus Virginiana pendula	Juniper, Weeping Red Cedar	1 00
119 Laurus Camphora	Camphor tree	1 50
120 **Libocedrus Chilensis**	Chilian Libocedrus	1 to 2 00
121 Libocedrus Decurrens	Californian Libocedrus	1 to 2 00
122 Libocedrus Doniana	Libocedrus, Don's	1 to 2 00

Picea Amabilis, *see Abies.*

6

	Botanical Name.	Common Name.	Price.
123	Magnolia grandiflora..............	Great flowered Magnolia..............	50 to 2 00
124	Magnolia Semiplena.............	Semidouble Magnolia.............	3 00
125	Magnolia Hartwicus..............	Hartweg's new evergreen Magnolia.....	5 00
126	Magnolia Oxoniensis (*Ferruginea*).....	Exmouth Magnolia.............	1 to 2 00
127	Magnolia Gallisonari.........	Angiers Magnolia.............	1 50
128	Magnolia Præcox.............	Early Flowering Magnolia.............	1 50
129	Magnolia Undulata.............	Waved-leaved Magnolia.............	50 to 2 00

N. B.—Some of the above of extra size, $3 to $5.

130	Olea Europea..............	Fruit-bearing Olive, four fine varieties...	1 to 2 00
131	Picea Balsamea.............	Balsam Fir.............	50
		Do., 5 to 14 feet.............	1 to 4 00
132	Picea Cephalonica.............	Cephalonian Fir.............	1 to 2 00
133	Picea Fraserii.............	Fraser's Balsam Fir.............	75 to 1 50
	Picea Grandis, see *Abies Douglassii*.		
134	Picea lasiocarpa.............	**Fir, Woolly-leaved.**	4 00
135	Picea Nobilis.............	Fir, Californian Noble.............	2 to 3 00
136	Picea Nordmaniana.............	Fir, or **Spruce, Nordman's.**	2 00
137	Picea Pectinata.............	Fir, or Spruce, European Silver......	50 to 1 00
138	Picea Pectinata compacta.............	Fir, or Spruce, Compact Silver.............	1 00
139	Picea Pindrow.............	Fir, or Spruce, Kumaon Pindrow.............	1 00
140	Picea Pichta—Sibirica.............	Fir, or Spruce, Siberian.............	1 00
141	Picea Pinsapo.............	Fir, or Spruce, Mount Atlas.............	1 50 to 2 00
143	Picea Webbiana (Spectabilis).............	Fir, or Spruce, Nepal purple-coned.....	1 50 to 2 00
144	Pinus Austriaca.............	**Pine, Austrian Black.**	50
		Do., 3 to 8 feet.............	1 to 4 00
145	Pinus Benthamiana.............	Pine, Bentham's Californian, splendid.....	75
146	Pinus Brutia.............	Pine, Brutia.............	1 00
147	Pinus Calabriensis.............	Pine, Calabrian, splendid.............	1 to 2 00
148	Pinus Cembra.............	Pine, Siberian Cembran, grows slow.....	1 00
149	Pinus cilicica.............	Pine, Cilicious.............	2 00
150	Pinus Coulterii.............	Pine, Great-hooked.............	2 00
151	Pinus Excelsa.............	Pine, Bhotan Lofty.............	50 to 2 00
152	Pinus Haguensis.............	Pine, Hagueneau.............	1 00
153	Pinus Halepensis.............	Pine, Aleppo.............	75
154	Pinus Insignis vera.............	Pine, Monterey.............	1 to 2 00
155	Pinus Jeffreyi.............	Pine, Jeffrey's Californian.............	2 to 3 00
156	Pinus Lambertiana.............	Pine, Lambert's gigantic.............	2 00
157	Pinus Laricio.............	Pine, Corsican.............	75
158	Pinus Macrocarpa, vel Sabiniana......	Pine, Sabine's Californian.............	3 00
159	Pinus Mitis.............	Pine, American yellow.............	1 00
160	Pinus Montezumæ.............	Pine, Montezuma.............	2 to 3 00
161	Pinus Montpeliensis.............	Pine, Montpelier.............	1 00
162	Pinus Monticola.............	Pine, Short-leaved Weymouth.............	1 00
163	Pinus Mughus, or Pumilio.............	Pine, Dwarf mountain.............	50 to 75
164	Pinus Palustris (*Australis*).............	Pine, Carolina pitch.............	1 to 2 00
165	Pinus Pineaster.............	Pine, Cluster coned.............	50 to 1 00
		Do., 4 to 8 feet.............	2 to 4 00
166	Pinus Pinea.............	Pine, Italian stone, (eatable nuts)...	75 to 1 50
167	Pinus Ponderosa.............	Pine, Oregon, heavy wood.............	2 00
168	Pinus Pungens.............	Pine, Spiny-coned.............	1 50
169	Pinus Resinosa.............	Pine, American red, long beautiful foliage	50 to 1 00
170	Pinus Rigensis.............	Pine, Riga.............	50
171	Pinus Rigida.............	Pine, Prickly-coned, or Pitch.............	50
172	Pinus Spiralis.............	Pine, Californian spiral.............	3 to 5 00
173	Pinus Strobus.............	Pine, White or Weymouth.............	50
174	Pinus Sylvestris.............	Pine, Scotch pine, or fir.............	50
175	Pinus Tuberculata.............	Pine, Californian tuberculate.............	1 00
176	Podocarpus Coreanus.............	Chinese Yew, Coreanus.............	1 00
177	Podocarpus Coriacea.............	Chinese Yew, Thick-leaved.............	75
178	Podocarpus Japonica.............	Japan Yew.............	1 50
179	Podocarpus Longifolius.............	Chinese Yew, Long-leaved.............	1 00
180	Podocarpus Mackii.............	Chinese Yew, Mackii.............	1 00
181	Podocarpus Macrophylla.............	Japan Yew, Large-leaved.............	1 00
182	Podocarpus Neriifolia.............	Chinese Yew, Oleander-leaved.............	1 00
183	Podocarpus Sinensis.............	Chinese Yew, Chinese Sylvan.............	1 00
184	Podocarpus Totara.............	Chinese Yew, Totara.............	1 00
185	Retinospora ericoides.............	Retinospora, Heath-leaved.............	50 to 1 00

Botanical Name.	Common Name.	Price.
186 Saxegothea conspicua	Showy Saxegothea	1 to 2 00
187 Taxodium Horsfalliæ (Evergreen)	Yew-leaved Cypress, Horsfall's	2 00
188 Taxodium Sempervirens (Evergreen)	Californian red wood (large size $2)	50 to 1 00
Taxodium (deciduous).	**Deciduous Cypress.**	
189 Taxodium Distichum	Deciduous Cypress, American	50
190 Taxodium Sinensis pendulum	Deciduous Cypress, Chinese Weeping	1 00
191 Taxus adpressa	Yew, Japan dark green	1 00
192 Taxus baccata	Yew, English	50 to 75
	Do., 3 to 6 feet, $1 per foot.	
193 Taxus Baccata variegata	Yew, Gold-striped	1 to 2 00
194 Taxus Canadensis	Yew, American Trailing	30 to 50
195 Taxus Dovastonii pendula	Yew, Weeping	75 to 1 50
196 Taxus Elegantissima	Yew, Elegant	75
197 Taxus Erecta, or Stricta	Yew, Erect	50 to 1 00
Do., 2 to 5 feet, $1 per foot.		
198 Taxus Ericoides	Yew, Heath leaved	75
199 Taxus Hibernica fastigiata	Yew, Irish spiral (2 to 4 feet, $1 per foot).	50
200 Taxus Imperialis	Yew, Imperial	2 00
N. B.—For other species, see *Cephalotaxus.*		
201 Thuya Asplenifolia	**Arbor Vitæ,** Fern-leaved	50
202 Thuya Aurea	Arbor Vitæ, Gold-tipped, beautiful	75 to 1 00
203 Thuya Australis	Arbor Vitæ, Australian	1 25
204 Thuya Californica	Arbor Vitæ, Californian dark green	1 to 2 00
205 Thuya compacta	Arbor Vitæ, Compact	1 00
206 Thuya Cupressoides	Arbor Vitæ, Cypress-like	2 00
207 Thuya Dolobrata	Arbor Vitæ, Dolobrata	1 to 2 00
Thuya Doniana, see *Libocedrus.*		
208 Thuya Gigantea (Menziesii)	Arbor Vitæ, Californian gigantic	50 to 1 00
209 Thuya Glauca (Biota)	Arbor Vitæ, Glaucous	75
210 Thuya incurvata	Arbor Vitæ, Incurved	1 50
211 Thuya Hybrida	Arbor Vitæ, Hybrid	1 00
212 Thuya Japonica	Arbor Vitæ, Japan	50 to 1 00
213 Thuya Lobii	Arbor Vitæ, Lobb's Californian	2 00
214 Thuya microcarpa	Arbor Vitæ, Small capsuled	1 50
215 Thuya nana	Arbor Vitæ, Dwarf	1 00
216 Thuya occidentalis compacta	Arbor Vitæ, Compact American	1 to 1 50
217 Thuya Nepalensis (Tartarica)	Arbor Vitæ, Nepal, or Tartarian	50 to 60
218 Thuya Occidentalis	Arbor Vitæ, American	25 to 50
Do., extra large and fine, 5 to 14 feet, $1 to $5.		
219 Thuya occidentalis variegata	Arbor Vitæ, Variegated	1 00
220 Thuya Orientalis	Arbor Vitæ, Chinese	25 to 50
221 Thuya Pendula filiformis	Arbor Vitæ, Weeping-thready	1 00
222 Thuya Plicata	Arbor Vitæ, Plaited-leaved	50 to 1 50
223 Thuya Sphæroidalis	Arbor Vitæ, Sphœroid	2 00
224 Thuya stricta	Arbor Vitæ, Upright	50
225 Thuya Sibirica	Arbor Vitæ, Siberian, very compact	75
Do., 2½ to 4 feet, $1 to $2 50.		
226 Thuya Warenna	Arbor Vitæ, Ware's new	50
227 Torreya myristicha	Torreya, Californian	6 00
228 Torreya nucifera	Torreya, Nutbearing	2 00
229 Torreya Taxifolia	Torreya, Yew-leaved	50 to 1 50
230 Thuiopsis boreale	Thuiopsis, Boreal	1 50
231 Washingtonia, or Sequoia Gigantea	Great Californian tree, 1 and 2 years	75 to 2 00

EVERGREEN SHRUBS.

N. B.—Extra large Shrubs can be supplied of many kinds, at proportionate rates.

Note.—Those which require to be protected in this latitude during the winter, by a covering of straw, are designated by an asterisk *.

1 Andromeda Axillaris major	**Andromeda,** Axillary flowered	75
2 Andromeda Floribunda	Andromeda, Profuse flowered	1 00
3 Andromeda polyfolia	Andromeda, Many-leaved	50
4 *Arbutus unedo	Evergreen Strawberry tree	75
5 *Arbutus Andrachne	Levant Strawberry tree	1 50

Botanical Name.	Common Name.	Price.
6 Ardisia Japonica, or Serrulata, hardy	Ardisia, Japan	40
7 *Ardisia Crenulata	Chinese Crenulate Ardisia	40
8 **Aucuba Japonica**	Japan Gold-dust tree (larger $1 to $1 50)	50
9 **Berberis Aruacensis**	Berberry, Aruaceneis	2 00
10 Berberis Bealii	Beale's Pinnate-leaved	1 75
11 *Berberis Darwinii	Patagonian Berberry	25 to 1 00
12 Berberis Fortunei. (See Mahonia)	Fortune's Chinese Berberry	1 00
13 Berberis Dulcis	Sweet-fruited Berberry	30
14 Berberis elegans	Beautiful Berberry	75
For other species of Berberis, see Mahonia.		
15 **Buxus** arborescens lancifolia	**Tree Box,** Lance-leaved, very hardy	25 to 1 00
16 Buxus Angustifolia	Tree Box, Narrow-leaved	25 to 1 00
17 Buxus Latifolia	Tree Box, Broad-leaved	25 to 1 00
18 Buxus Myrtifolia	Tree Box, Myrtle-leaved	1 00
19 Buxus Argentea variegata	Tree Box, Silver-striped	25 to 1 00
20 Buxus Aurea marginata	Tree Box, Gold edged	50 to 1 00
N. B.—Plants of the 6 above varieties, 2 to 6 feet, $1 to $8.		
21 Buxus Aurea maculata	Tree Box, Gold-blotched	1 00
22 Buxus Balearica	Tree Box, Minorca	1 00
23 Buxus Glauca	Tree Box, Glaucous-leaved	50
24 Buxus Thymifolia	Tree Box, Thyme-leaved	75
25 Buxus Suffruticosa	Dwarf Box, for borders. See page 30	25
26 *Camellia Japonica	**Camellia,** Japan, 250 splendid varieties.	
27 Cerasus Laurocerasus	English Laurel	25 to 50
28 Cerasus Lusitanica	Portugal Laurel	50
29 *Cleyera Japonica	Japan Cleyera	1 50
30 **Cotoneaster** Buxifolia	**Cotoneaster,** Box-leaved	30 to 40
31 Cotoneaster Marginata	Cotoneaster, Margined	50
32 Cotoneaster Rotundifolia	Cotoneaster, Round-leaved	50
33 Cotoneaster Microphylla	Small-leaved Cotoneaster	30 to 40
34 Cotoneaster Thymifolia	Thyme-leaved Cotoneaster, and others	30 to 40
35 **Crataegus** crenulata	Crenulate-leaved Thorn	1 50
36 Crataegus Pyracantha	Fiery Thorn	30 to 50
37 *Daphne Indica	**Daphne,** Chinese fragrant	50
83 *Daphne Argentea	Daphne, Silver-striped, red flowered	75
93 Daphne Japonica	Daphne, Japan	1 00
40 **Eleagnus** Crispa	Oleaster, or Wild Olive, Curl-leaved	1 00
41 Eleagnus Argentea	Oleaster, Silvery-leaved	50
42 Eleagnus Reflexa	Oleaster, Japan reflex-leaved	1 00
43 **Erica** vulgaris, &c.	Scotch Heather, eight varieties	50
44 Eriobotrya Japonica	Japan Medlar, splendid foliage	50 to 1 00
45 Escallonia floribunda	**Escallonia,** Profuse-flowered	50
46 Escallonia macrantha	Escallonia, Large-leaved	30
47 Escallonia rubra, &c.	Escallonia, Red flowering	25
48 **Euonymus** Japonicus	**Euonymus,** Japan green	25 to 35
49 Euonymus Argentea	Euonymus, Japan Silver-striped	25 to 35
50 Euonymus Aurea	Euonymus, Japan Gold-striped	50
51 Euonymus Fimbriatus	Euonymus, Chinese laurel-leaved	1 00
52 Euonymus Rosmarinifolia	Euonymus, Rosemary-leaved	50
53 Euonymus Europeus nanus	Euonymus, Dwarf	50
Genista, see Spartium.		
54 **Hedera** arborescens	Tree Ivy	50
55 **Helianthemum** apeninum	**Helianthemum,** Alpine	50
56 **Ilex** Aquifolium	Holly, European	50 to 1 00
Do., 3 to 5 feet, $2 50 to $4.		
57 Ilex Argentea	Holly, Silver striped	50 to 1 00
58 Ilex Aurea	Holly, Gold-striped	75 to 1 00
59 Ilex Balearica	Holly, Minorca large-leaved, beautiful	1 to 1 50
60 Ilex Buxifolia	Holly, Box-leaved	1 00
61 Ilex Cassine	Holly, Cassine, small leaved	75
62 Ilex Canadensis	Holly, Canadian	50
63 Ilex Cornuta	Holly, Chinese Cornute, splendid	3 00
64 Ilex Crassifolia	Holly, Thick-leaved	1 00
65 Ilex Dipyrena	Holly, Dipyrena	2 00
66 Ilex Ferox	Holly, Green Hedgehog	75
67 Ilex Ferox variegata	Holly, Striped leaved Hedgehog	1 00
68 Ilex Furcata	Holly, Chinese Furcate	3 00
69 Ilex Hibernica	Holly, Irish, dark green	1 00

Botanical Name.	Common Name.	Price.
70 Ilex Japonica latifolia.................	Holly, Japan broad leaved............	1 50 to 2 00
71 Ilex Laurifolia.....................	Holly, Laurel leaved................	1 00
72 Ilex Marginata alba................	Holly, White-edged................	75
73 Ilex Marginata aurea...............	Holly, Gold-edged.................	75
74 Ilex Myrtifolia....................	Holly, Myrtle leaved...............	1 00
75 Ilex Paraguensis...................	Holly, Paraguay Tea...............	2 00
76 Ilex Perado.......................	Holly, Madeira thick-leaved..........	1 50
77 Ilex Scottica.....................	Holly, Scotch pale green............	50 to 1 00
78 Ilex Serratifolia..................	Holly, Serrated leaved	75
79 Ilex Tarago of Japan..............	Holly, Japan Tarago, splendid foliage....	2 to 3 00
80 Ilex Vomitoria...................	Holly, Yapan Tea.................	1 00
81 *Illicium floridanum.............	Aniseed Tree, Purple-flowered.........	40 to 1 00
82 *Illicium Japonicum..............	Aniseed Tree, Japan yellow..........	1 00
83 *Illicium Parviflorum............	Aniseed Tree, Small-flowered..........	1 00
84 *Illicium Religiosum.............	Aniseed Tree, Chinese sacred.........	50 to 1 00
85 Juniperus prostrata (depressa).....	Juniper, depressed................	50
86 Kalmia latifolia.................	Laurel, American.................	50
87 Kalmia latifolia Nivea............	Laurel, Snow white...............	2 00
88 Kalmia angustifolia..............	Laurel, Narrow-leaved.............	50
89 *Laurus regalis.................	Laurel, Californian Bay, fragrant.......	1 00
90 *Laurus Nobilis.................	Laurel, Sweet Bay, or Apollo's Laurel...	35 to 1 00
91 Laurus undulata................	Laurel, Wave-leaved..............	1 00
92 Lavendula spica................	Lavendar......................	25
93 Ledum latifolium...............	Ledum, Broad-leaved.............	50
94 Leycesteria formosa.............	Showy Leycesteria...............	50
95 Ligustrum italicum (sempervirens)...	Privet, Evergreen................	25
96 *Ligustrum Japonicum............	Privet, Chinese.................	30 to 50

N. B.—The following is a most beautiful and unique family of Evergreens, with profuse clusters of spring flowers. Extra size plants, $2 to $3.

97 Mahonia Aquifolia...............	Mahonia, Holly-leaved.............	25 to 50
98 Mahonia Diversifolia.............	Mahonia, Diverse-leaved...........	1 00
99 Mahonia Fascicularis............	Mahonia, Californian shining-leaved.....	25 to 50
100 Mahonia Fortunei..............	Mahonia, Fortune's Chinese.........	1 00
101 Mahonia Glumacea.............	Mahonia, Dwarf Glumaceous..........	75
102 Mahonia Intermedia............	Mahonia, Intermediate............	1 00
103 Mahonia Japonica.............	Mahonia, Japan pinnate............	1 50
104 Mahonia Nepalensis...........	Mahonia, Nepal large-leaved.........	1 50
105 Mahonia Repens..............	Mahonia, Creeping-rooted..........	50
106 Mahonia Rotundifolia..........	Mahonia, Round-leaved............	1 00
107 *Mahonia Tenuifolia...........	Mahonia, Narrow-leaved...........	1 50
108 *Mahonia Trifoliata...........	Mahonia, Trifoliate..............	1 50
109 Myrica cerifera..............	Wax Myrtle, fragrant.............	38
110 Neillia thyrsiflora............	Thyrse-flowered Neillia............	75
111 Olea fragrans................	Olive, Chinese Fragrant............	38 to 1 00
112 Olea Major latifolia...........	Olive, Chinese large-leaved.........	1 50
113 Photinia Californica..........	Photinia, Californian Laurel-leaved.....	2 00
114 Photinia dentata.............	Photinia, Dentate-leaved..........	1 00
115 Photinia Serrulata...........	Photinia, Glossy dark leaved........	1 00
116 *Phillyrea angustifolia........	Phillyrea, Narrow-leaved..........	50
117 *Phillyrea Latifolia..........	Phillyrea, Broad-leaved...........	50
118 *Phillyrea Media............	Phillyrea, Intermediate...........	50
119 *Phillyrea Oleafolia..........	Phillyrea, Olive-leaved...........	50
120 *Phillyrea Serratafolia........	Phillyrea, Serrate-leaved..........	75
121 *Pittosporum tobira..........	Pittosporum, Chinese Fragrant.......	35
122 *Pittosporum tobira variegata....	Pittosporum, Chinese striped........	40
123 *Pittosporum Undulatum.......	Pittosporum, Waved-leaved.........	50 to 75
124 *Pittosporum Undulatum variegata....	Pittosporum, Striped Wave-leaved......	1 00
125 Quercus Ilex................	Oak, English Evergreen............	1 00
126 Quercus Suber..............	Oak, Spanish Cork..............	1 00
127 Rhamnus crocea.............	Californian Buckthorn............	2 00
128 Rhamnus Alaturnus..........	Broad-leaved Alaturnus...........	1 00
129 Rosmarinus officinalis........	Rosemary....................	25
130 Ruscus aculeatus...........	Butcher's Broom, singular..........	75
131 Ruta graveolens............	Rue, herb...................	25
132 Skimmia Japonica..........	Japan Skimmia...............	2 00
133 Spartium scoparium........	Scotch Broom................	25

Do., large, 5 to 7 feet, 50 cts. to $1.

Botanical Name.	Common Name.	Price.
134 Ilex europeus, pleno............	Double Whin, or Furze............	50
135 *Viburnum tinus............	Laurustinus,............	38
136 *Viburnum Japonicum	**Viburnum, Japan**............	75
137 *Viburnum Lucidum	Viburnum, Shining-leaved........	50
138 *Viburnum Macrocephalum.......	Viburnum, Chinese Snowball......	2 00
139 *Viburnum Odoratissimum.........	Viburnum, Fragrant............	50
140 *Viburnum Plicatum............	Viburnum, Chinese Plicate.......	50
141 *Yucca Aloefolia............	**Adam's Needle,** Aloe-leaved....	50
142 Yucca Angustifolia...........	Adam's Needle, Narrow-leaved.....	1 00
143 Yucca Filamentosa...........	Adam's Needle, Thready-leaved.....	25 to 50
144 Yucca variegata............	Adam's Needle, Striped-leaved.....	1 00
145 Yucca Flaccida............	Adam's Needle, Profuse-flowered...	75
146 Yucca Gloriosa............	Adam's Needle, Erect............	50 to 1 00
147 Yucca Recurvifolia.........	Adam's Needle, Reflexed leaved....	50

------ • ◆ • ------

RHODODENDRON, OR ROSE BAY.

Catawbiense............	1 00	McDowell's American............	2 00
Maximum roseum.....	75 to 1 00	Ponticum............	50 to 1 00

Hardy Grafted Varieties, $1 50 to $2 each.

Album (Ponticum).	Dauricum.	Maculatum.
Album elegans.	Delicatum.	Macranthon.
Album grandiflorum.	Delicatissimum.	Maximum album.
Andersonii.	Everstianum.	Multimaculatum.
Angustifolium.	Ferrugineum.	Murillo.
Angustus.	Georgiana.	Ne plus ultra.
Aureum variegatum (gold-	Giganteum.	Nigrum.
striped.	Glennyanum.	Nivaticum.
Azureum.	Gloriosum.	Pictum.
Bicolor.	Glory of Flushing.	Ponticum roseum.
Blandum.	Grandiflorum.	Ponticum plenum.
Candidissimum.	Gullatum.	Purpureum elegans.
Caucassicum.	Hannibal.	Roseum elegans.
Cato.	Henry Drummond.	Roseum pictum.
Celestinum.	Hyacinthiflorum.	Speciosum.
Celestinum frictum.	Lee's Deep Maroon.	Splendens.
Cerulescens.	Lucidum.	Superbum.

N. B.—Some Rhododendrons of extra size, 4 to 6 feet, $3 to $5 each.

------ • ------

RHODODENDRONS—REQUIRING PROTECTION.

Arboreum and Hybrids, 22 splendid varieties, | Sikkim Himalaya, 10 splendid varieties, $2 to $3.
$1 to $2.

------ • ◆ • ------

SELECTIONS OF EVERGREEN TREES AND SHRUBS.

The Norway Spruce, as a beautiful broad conical tree, of extreme hardihood, and suited to almost any location, commands universal approbation. The Drooping variety, interspersed with the Upright growing one, presents an agreeable contrast. The European White and American White Spruces are still more beautiful, and assume a more spiral and less spreading form, as they advance in growth. The Hemlock, or Weeping Spruce, when allowed to branch from the ground, with ample space for expansion, is one of our most graceful trees. There are many other Spruces of great beauty, but, being more rare, they are not obtainable of sufficiently large size for immediate embellishment.

Of the Cedars, the most beautiful is the Silvery-leaved Deodar, of graceful form, with drooping branches, and of very rapid growth. Some trees of this species were partially injured here during the unprecedented winter of 55–56; but they have regained their vigor; and we may rest assured that, when such trees shall have attained size and strength, they will withstand the climate perfectly, and further to the South they will, of course, be permanently secure, even when of the smallest size. The deep-green Deodar forms a more spiral tree, of great beauty, and has proved itself the hardiest of its class, and is also of rapid growth. On this account it is destined to take precedence of the Cedar of Lebanon, whose growth is comparatively slow, with branches much more spreading. Among the species of Cypress, the most lofty and beautiful are the Pyramidalis and Expansa, so noted for ornamenting the cemeteries of Oriental Countries and of the south of Europe. These two are well suited to localities south of Washington, but are often injured severely in this latitude.

The most desirable Pines are the White and Red Pines of our own Country, and the Austrian, Pincaster, Scotch, Calabrian, Bhotan, and Cembran, and the Bentham, Sabine, and Spiral Californian Pines. Of the Junipers the most symmetrical and conical are the Silvery leaved, Irish, and Swedish,—all of the most hardy character, capable of sustaining the severest northern winters. The Chinese is also quite ornamental, though attaining only a moderate height; but the Carolina Conical Juniper, or Cedar, will reach a height of thirty feet, with a beautiful head. The splendid Cryptomerias of Japan, with their most graceful drooping foliage, sustain our winters here, but will not succeed further to the north. The American, Siberian, and Chinese Arbor Vitæ are all well suited for general adornment, and also for screens and hedges. The last two do not attain to an equal size with the former. Of the Yew family the English Upright, English Spreading, and the Irish, are the principal species of interest; the former is much the most desirable, and grows more rapidly than any other of its class.

The Magnolia grandiflora and its varieties produce the most splendid flowers of all the Evergreen family; and, by binding them in straw, we have preserved fine trees, now of twenty years' growth.

Evergreen Shrubs.—The most desirable are the Mahonias and Rhododendrons, for their splendid foliage and profusion of bloom, the Aucuba, the various Hollies, Euonymus, Cotoneasters, Phillyreas, and Photinias, and the Tree Box of the different varieties, for the beauty of their foliage, and for permanent ornament during winter, when they serve so greatly to cheer and enliven the "Winter Garden."

------ • ◄◆► • ------

TREES AND SHRUBBERY SUITABLE FOR CEMETERIES.

Ash, Mountain.
European Weeping.
Golden Weeping.
White fringed.
Curled-leaved, dark green.
Arbor Vitæ, American.
Californian.
Chinese.
Siberian.
Aucuba Japonica.
Beech, Purple-leaved.
Green Weeping.
Bignonia crucigera, Evergreen climber.
Berberry, Purple-leaved.
Box Dwarf, for edging.
Tree, green, and variegated.
Cedar of Lebanon.
Cedrus Deodora.
Cherry Weeping.
Cryptomeria Japonica (Weeping)
Cupressus Funebris (Funebral Cypress).

Eglantine, several varieties.
Euonymus, Japan green.
Japan Variegated.
European white berried.
European pink   do
European scarlet   do
European crimson berried.
Holly, European green, six varieties.
Variegated, eight varieties.
Scotch and Irish.
Ilex, Balearica, beautiful foliage.
Ivy, Irish large-leaved, ⎫ Climb-
English small do ⎬ ers.
Poetic,   ⎭
Jasmine, several species.
Juniper, Irish dark green.
Argentea, Silvery.
Swedish light green.
Oblonga pendula(Weeping)
Kalmia latifolia.
Laurel, English, or Apollo's.
Portugal.

Laurel, Alexandrian or Classic, an Evergreen Climber.
Linden, Scarlet Twig.
Weeping.
Magnolia, various species.
Mahonia, several beautiful species.
Purple Fringe-tree.
Rhododendron, numerous splendid varieties.
Vinca, or Running Myrtle, ⎫
9 varieties.   ⎪
Virginia Creeper.   ⎪
Virgin's Bower, or Clematis, ⎬ Climbers.
10 species.   ⎪
Wistaria, Chinese Blue. ⎪
White or Snowy.   ⎭
Willow, Weeping Ring-leaved.
Woodbine, several species,Climbers.
Yew, English spreading.
English upright.
Irish.

CHINESE TREE PÆONIES.—PÆONIA MOUTAN.

These are the most splendid and showy of all Flowering Shrubs, and among the most rare.

The flowers are mostly fragrant, and all are double, unless denoted otherwise. They are perfectly hardy, and will withstand the winters of our most northern States and the Canadas. They bloom in May, ten to fifteen days before the Chinese Herbaceous varieties.

Extra large plants of five and six years' growth, of Nos. 1 and 2, can be supplied at $3 each; and also of many other varieties, at $3, and others at $5 and upwards.

Those marked thus * are Seedlings originated by W. R. Prince.

There is no other extensive Collection of this Class of Plants in the Union; and those we supply are far larger plants than are usually sold, and of blooming age. They are mostly on their own roots, and but few are grafted.

Botanical Name.	Description.	Price.
1 BANKSII	Roseate, very large, magnificent, protuberant, fragrant.	75 to 1 00
DITTO	Larger size	2 00
2 PAPAVERACEA	Very large, single white, with crimson center	75 to 1 00
DITTO	Larger size	2 00

Botan caliName.	Description.	Price.
3 Lilacina Carnea......................	Lilac blush, crimson center, semi double..	1 50
4 Maxima plena.......................	Large, Rosy blush, fragrant,............	2 to 3 00

Note.—We have a great stock of strong plants of the above four varieties, which we will sell low by dozen or hundred.

The following twenty-one splendid varieties were originated from seeds by Wm. R. Prince:—

5 *Banksii Pallida plenissima............	Very large, pale roseate, splendid, protuberant, becomes nearly white.......	3 00
6 *Banksii Coronata plenissima..........	Coronet flowered, deep rosy crimson....	3 to 5 00
7 *Banksii Purpurascens minor..........	Purplish crimson, minor Banksian.......	2 to 3 00
8 *Banksii Rosacea plenissima...........	Roseate Banksian, very fine............	2 to 3 00
9 *Banksii Purpurea pallida.............	Large, pale purple................	5 00
10 *Banksii Rosea superba...............	Large, rose colored, full double........	6 00
11 *Incarnata Splendida................	Large, blush incarnate, changing to white, lilac centre, full double,...........	8 00
12 *Papaveracea rosea pallida....	Imperial, Poppy flowered.............	5 00
13 *Papaveracea Elegans................	Rosy purple, blush border, beautiful....	5 00
14 *Papaveracea Purpurea pallida........	Large, pale purple, deeper center.......	5 00
15 *Papaveracea Bicolor superba.........	Large, White, crimson center, full double, extra.....................	6 00
16 *Papaveracea Incarnata...............	Large, rosy incarnate, golden stamens, beautiful, distinct................	6 00
17 *Papaveracea Rosea pallida...........	Large, blush, semi-double.............	4 00
18 *Papaveracea Alba striata............	Large white, each petal strongly marked with crimson extending to the center.	8 00
19 *Papaveracea Rosea striata...........	Rosy, distinct crimson, striped from center	6 00
20 *Princesse........................	Monstrous, rosy lilac, splendid..........	5 00
21 *Rosea Carminea plena...............	Rosy Carmine, the strongest growth of all the varieties.................	5 00
22 *Rosea Sanguinea minor..............	Small, deep rosy crimson, protuberant, fine	5 00
23 *Rosetta.........................	Large, purplish Banksian.............	5 00
24 *Rosalind........................	Pale rosy lilac, golden stamens, fine......	5 00
25 *Sylvania.........................	Very large, pale lilac, deep purple center.	5 00

The following are imported varieties. We can supply extra size plants of most of the varieties, at a moderate advance in prices.

26 Alba plena........................	Belgian white, crimson center..........	1 50
27 Alba variegata.....................	White variegated...................	1 50 to 2 50
28 Amabilis.........................	Lovely flowers.....................	1 50 to 2 00
29 Arethusa.........................	White, center bright crimson..........	1 50 to 2 50
30 Atroviolacea......................	Violet shaded.....................	1 50
31 Carmosina plenissima...............	Incarnate, full, fine................	3 00
32 Carlii...........................	White, purple center...............	1 50
33 Carnea plena......................	Fine incarnate....................	1 50
34 Caroline.........................	Caroline.........................	2 00
35 Cericea purpurea, vel superba........	Purplish Cherry, splendid............	1 50 to 3 00
36 Chauverii........................	Very large, blush lilac...............	1 50 to 2 50
37 Compte de Flandres.................	Rosy lilac.......................	2 00
38 Compte de Niepperg.................	....	1 50 to 2 50
39 De Bugny........................	Pearly blush white, purple center.......	1 50
40 Delachei.........................	....	1 50
41 Dionysii..........................	....	2 to 3 00
42 Elizabeth.........................	Bright red, splendid................	5 00
43 Fragrans maxima...................	Very large, fine odor,..............	5 00
44 Fulgida..........................	....	2 50 to 3 00
45 Giganten.........................	....	2 to 2 50
46 Gunoperi.........................	....	1 50 to 2 50
47 Grand Duke of Baden................	....	1 50
48 Heldii............................	Blush White, center shaded, purple......	1 50
49 Hissiana..........................	White, purple center................	1 50
50 Homei d'Italie......................	Hume's Italian....................	5 00
51 Imperatrice de France...............	....	5 00
52 Imperatrice Josephine...............	Large, purple, deeper center...........	2 00
53 Incarnata plena....................	Rosy incarnate, beautiful............	2 to 3 00
54 Kaehlini..........................	Large red........................	3 00
55 Le Feveriana......................	....	1 50 to 2 50
56 Le Soleil.........................	Pale roseate, imbricated..............	1 50 to 2 00

Botanical Name.	Description.	Price.
57 Leoliense	Blush white, crimson center	1 50
58 Lilacina major plenissima	Blush lilac, full center	1 50
59 Louise Mouchelet		3 00
60 Madame Laffay		1 50
61 Mammoth		3 to 1 50
62 Maxima rosea staminea	Large, roseate, some stamens	2 50
63 Mirabilis		1 50 to 2 50
64 Mirbellu	Rosy blush, purple center	3 00
65 Muhlenbeckii		1 50
66 Neumannii	Newman's Carmine, splendid	1 50 to 3 00
67 Ocellata		1 50
68 Ottonis vel Regia	Rosy crimson, not full, beautiful	1 50
69 Papaveracea alba	Large, white, deep center	2 to 2 50
70 Papaveracea rubra		1 50 to 2 50
71 Papaveracea carnea	Pale roseate, beautiful	3 00
72 Papaveracea plena	Bicolor Poppy, flowered	5 00
73 Parmentieri		1 50 to 2 50
74 Phœnicea	Phœnicean	1 50 to 2 50
75 Plenissima lilacina major	Large lilac, very double	5 00
76 Prince de Wagram	Roseate, crimson center	1 50
77 Purpurea	Violet purple	3 to 4 50
78 Purpurea plena undulata	Purple, undulated	5 00
79 Remembrance of Downing		3 50
80 Rienzi	Blush roseate, crimson center, fine, distinct	3 00
81 Roi des Crises	Bright Cherry colored	1 50 to 2 50
82 Rosa Gallica	Bright crimson, not full	2 to 4 00
83 Rosa mundi		1 50
84 Rosa odorata Phœnicea	Phœnican, rose color	3 00
85 Rosea superba	Beautiful roseate	1 50
86 Roseaformis	Large, rose form	1 50 to 3 00
87 Rosea odorata	Rosy carmine, very large, semi-double, weak growth	1 50 to 3 00
88 Roseolens odorata	Rose colored, fragrant	1 50
89 Rubané de Flandres	Striped, splendid	8 00
90 Rubra plena	Fine red	1 50 to 2 50
91 Savii	Blush white, center purple shaded	1 50
92 Schultessii	Deep pink, center rosy crimson	1 50
93 Schultessii lasciniata		1 50 to 2 50
94 Speciosissima	Purplish crimson	1 50
95 Splendens	Rosy crimson, pale shaded, protuberant. fragrant, extra	5 00
96 Splendidissima	Magnificent	5 00
97 Vandermaeli (Triomphe de)	Monstrous, pale blush, center rosy purple, full, splendid	2 to 3 00
98 Van Houttei	Bright carmine, splendid	3 to 4 00
99 Victoria alba	White, peculiar foliage	1 50
100 Violacea purpurea	Violet purple	1 50 to 3 50
101 Violacea superba nova	Superb violet	1 50 to 3 00
102 Walnerii	Blush white, center lilac	1 50 to 2 50

N. B.—Twenty-seven other splendid varieties are in course of propagation for our next Catalogue.

The following are distinct New Chinese Varieties obtained by Robert Fortune; and as they are the most rare and valuable varieties, the prices will be regulated according to their size.

1 Atropurpurea.	8 Cornelia.	15 Pride of Hong Kong.
2 Atrosanguinea.	9 Dr. Bowring.	16 Purpurea.
3 Beauty of Canton.	10 Globosa.	17 Reevesiana.
4 Berenice.	11 Ida.	18 Robert Fortune.
5 Bijou de Chusan.	12 Jewel of Chusan.	19 Salmonea.
6 Colonel Malcolm.	13 Lord Macartney.	20 Sir George Stanton.
7 Confucius.	14 Osiris.	21 Zenobia.

SPLENDID CHINESE HERBACEOUS DOUBLE PÆONIES.

These are varieties of Pæonia Sinensis, with the exception of No. 97. They are mostly very fragrant, and form the most brilliant appendage of the garden at their season of flowering, which is in June. They are of the most easy culture, prefer a northern exposure, and will support the severest Canadian winters, the most of the species being natives of Siberia and Chinese Tartary, and none of them from warm latitudes. We supply blooming roots, and not mere slips, such as are frequently sold ; and the prices are much below the usual rates, our stock being by far the largest in the Union.

ADDITIONAL CHINESE HERBACEOUS VARIETIES.

The following comprise the celebrated *Parmentier* Collection of Chinese Herbaceous Paeonies.

Chinese Herbaceous Pæonies—Rejected—being superseded by superior varieties of the same colors ·

Amabilis.	Elegantissima.	Papillionacea.
Claptoniana.	Glauca flore pleno.	Pomponia.
Delicatissima.	Lilacina plena.	Rosea Mutabilis.
Diversifolia.	Lilacina superba.	Striata Rosea alba
Elegans.	Lutea rosea.	Sulphurea alba.

DOUBLE HERBACEOUS PÆONIES—VARIOUS SPECIES.

These bloom in the month of May, about two weeks before the Chinese varieties. They are perfectly hardy.

OFFICINALIS PLENA.

181 Alba plena.............................Large white.......................... 1 00
182 Anemonaeflora.......................Deep crimson, large, anemone-form with crimson and golden stamens, extra, very distinct.......................... 1 00
183 Aurea ligustrata....................Bright deep crimson, anemone-form, long golden ligules.......................... 1 50
184 Atrofulgens...........................Brilliant crimson.......................... 1 50
185 Blanda plena.........................Pearly blush, nearly white, beautiful, rare.... 1 50
186 Etoile de Pluto......................Star of Pluto, very dark.......................... 75
188 La Mauvasse...2 00
189 L'Oriflamme.........................Brilliant banner.......................... 75
190 Maxima rosea.......................Large bright roseate.......................... 50
191 Noble pourpre........................Noble purple.......................... 75
192 Rubra plena..........................Dark crimson.......................... 25
193 Rosea pallida, Albicans or Carnescens...Incarnate changeable.......................... 38
194 Striata elegans......................Elegant striped flowers.......................... 2 00
195 Variegata..............................Variegated-leaved, roseate.......................... 1 00

PARADOXA PLENA.

201 Amaranthescens spherica..........Globose Amaranth, small flower, very tall.... 75
202 Erigone................................Erigone.......................... 75
203 Eureka, or Ourika..................Eureka.......................... 1 25
204 Fimbriata plena.....................Purple fringed.......................... 50
205 La Brillante..........................Brilliant.......................... 2 00
206 La negresse..........................Negress.......................... 1 25
207 Nana plena............................Dwarf.......................... 75
208 Nemesis................................Nemesis.......................... 75
209 Pompadoura...........................Deep purple.......................... 75
210 Pomponia striata....................Striped Pompone.......................... 2 00
211 Pomponia violacea..................Violet Pompone.......................... 1 00
212 Proserpine............................Purple.......................... 1 50
213 Pulchella plena......................Elegant purple.......................... 75
214 Rubescens plena...2 00
215 Rubra striata........................Red striped.......................... 2 00
216 Singuinea plena.....................Deep purplish crimson, superb.......................... 75
217 Tenuifolia plena.....................Crimson Fennel-leaved, early, beautiful...... 75
218 Violacea fimbriate plena...........Violet fringed.......................... 1 00
219 Violacea spherica...................Spherical violet.......................... 75

HERBACEOUS PÆONIES. SINGLE FLOWERING, OF DIFFERENT SPECIES.

These, like the preceding classes, are very hardy. Their period of bloom is the month of May.

225 Albiflora Sibirica	Siberian white cluster	25
226 Albiflora candida	White, glossy-leaved	50
227 Albiflora marginata	White, petals edged with pink, new	1 00
228 Albiflora vestalis	Siberian Virgin, white	50
229 Multiflora rosea	Siberian pearly blush cluster	50
230 Rubescens	Siberian blush-colored	50
231 Andersonii	Anderson's Blush, early	50
232 Arietina	Ramshorn, deep crimson	50
233 Decora elatior	Tall purplish crimson	50
234 Decora præcox	Early, broad-leaf, purplish crimson	50
235 Hybrida Caucasica	Hybrid Caucasian	38
236 Humilis latifolia	Spanish, violet roseate	20
237 Officinalis Sabini	Crimson officinal, large, golden stamens	75
238 Paradoxa simplici	Tall, violet roseate	50
239 Paradoxa Smouti	Bright violet	35
240 Russi	Russ' Sicilian crimson	1 00
241 Splendens or Fulgens	Large, bright crimson, short yellow and red stamens	1 00
242 Tartarica	Tartarian blush	50
243 Tenuifolia	Fennel-leaved, purplish crimson	38
244 Tenuifolia latifolia	Broad Fennel-leaved crimson	50
245 Humilis angustifolia	Spanish narrow-leaved	38

CHINESE AND OTHER HERBACEOUS PÆONIES.
Reduced Prices for Assortments.

When any 12 varieties are taken, selected by the purchaser, 15 per cent. discount.
When any 25 varieties are taken, selected by the purchaser, 20 per cent. discount.
When any 50 varieties are taken, selected by the purchaser, 25 per cent. discount.
Where 50 varieties are taken, half selected by the purchaser, 30 per cent. discount.
Where 100 plants are taken of 50 varieties, half selected by the purchaser, 85 per cent. discount.

Our Selection.—12 Chinese, very fine double varieties for $4; 12 fine varieties, more rare, for $5; 25 fine varieties for $8; 12 good varieties for $3.

GENERAL REMARKS.

Persons who may not have our whole set of Catalogues, or those of the latest edition, may, from not seeing some articles enumerated therein, infer that we cannot supply them. We have, therefore, to state, that we obtain all desirable new Fruit and Ornamental Trees, Shrubs and Plants, with the greatest dispatch, and are always among the first to have them for sale, whether announced in our Catalogues or not.

CANDID ADVICE TO AMATEURS.

We make it a point to cultivate the largest stock of all the most estimable varieties, and consequently have larger and finer trees of these kinds. If, therefore, those persons who are desirous of adorning with promptitude their gardens and pleasure grounds, will transmit to us a general list of their wants, and leave the selection in some degree to us, we will send strong, well grown specimen trees of the respective kinds, such as will be sure to succeed and realize their expectations.

NEW AND SUPERIOR ROSES.

We have obtained from France, Belgium, and England all the new Roses that have been latterly brought to notice, comprising such as have been announced in various European and American periodicals; and we shall announce them in our forthcoming "*Catalogue of New Roses.*" In the mean time we will furnish them to applicants.

SPLENDID BULBOUS FLOWERS, ETC.

The collection is very large, and comprises all the choice varieties of Hyacinths, Tulips, Japan and all other Lilies of 70 species and varieties. Crown Imperials, Fritillaries, Bulbocodium, Jonquils, Polyanthus Narcissus, Double and Single Narcissus, Crocus, Gladiolus, Snowdrop, Snowflake, Iris, Ornithogalum, Scilla, Allium, Ranunculus, Anemone, Cyclamen, Amaryllis, Ixia, Lachenalia, Zephyranthes, Oxalis, Gladiolus, Antholyza, Alstroemeria, Arum, Colchicum, Brunsvigia, Calochortus, Crinum, Dens Canis, Ferarin, Hæmanthus, Pancratium, Tuberose, &c., &c., besides DAHLIAS, 300 splendid varieties.

Every class will be supplied at very moderate rates, with a large discount to venders. All the details as to prices, descriptions, &c., will be found in Catalogues No. 2 and 9, and in a new one now preparing for publication.

POLYANTHUS, COWSLIP, PRIMROSE AND AURICULA.

We have made this lovely Family of Flowers a speciality, and have concentrated above 150 named varieties from England, France, and Belgium, which we shall publish ere long. In the mean time, we will send a *Written Catalogue* of them to amateurs who may desire it.

HERBACEOUS FLOWERING PLANTS.

Of this class of plants, our collection is so rich and extensive, and the new acquisitions so frequent and numerous, that we shall publish the *additions* in a distinct Catalogue. A very large assortment was comprised in the 42d edition of our Catalogue No. 2, to which amateurs can refer. Our present collection comprises not only all those usually found in other Catalogues, but several hundred rare Species and Varieties which are not in any other American collection, all of which will be supplied at the lowest rates. The assortments of the following are very extensive :—Carnations, Picotees, Phlox, Iris, Chrysanthemum, Verbena, Hemerocallis, Double Hollyhock, Polyanthus, Primrose, Cowslip, Auricula, Daisies, Funkia, Lychnis, Pansies, Hibiscus, Ledum, &c.

SUMMER FLOWERING PLANTS, FOR BEDDING AND BORDERS.

A very extensive and select assortment of the most rare and beautiful species, many of which are entirely new. They are enumerated in Catalogues Nos. 2 and 9.

GREENHOUSE PLANTS.

Assortments of the Camellia Japonica, the collection of which comprises 250 splendid varieties, and of Chinese Azalea, Fuchsia, Geranium, Achimenes, Nerium, Cineraria, Myrtle, Orange, Lemon, Citron, Acacia, Calceolaria, Passiflora, Gloxinia, Gladiolus, Amaryllis, Cactus, Erica, and of all other desirable genera, will be supplied at the lowest rates.

FRUIT AND ORNAMENTAL TREE SEEDS, ETC.

Apple, Pear, Peach, Cherry, Plum, Apricot, Quince, Grape, and other Fruit Seeds, can be supplied in quantities. Also Seeds of Pines, Spruces, and many other Evergreen Trees, and of many Deciduous Trees and Shrubs, and Flowering Plants. Orders for any of these should be given if possible in advance of the season for obtaining them.

AMERICAN SEEDS AND PLANTS FOR EUROPE.

Collections of Seeds of American Forest Trees and Shrubs, and of rare and beautiful American Plants, will be supplied, suitable to send to Europe and other countries.

AGRICULTURAL, GARDEN, AND FLOWER SEEDS.

The Catalogue in this department is very extensive, and we announce to all venders of Seeds that we will supply every variety desired at low wholesale rates, our desire being to present great inducements to those who will make prompt or sure arrangements as to payment. We also supply them put up in a superior manner, in retail parcels, at $30 to $40 per 1000 parcels.

STOCKS FOR ENGRAFTING.

Apple, Pear, Plum, Cherry, Mahaleb, Paradise and Doucin Apples, Angers and Paris Quinces, Manetti Rose, Althea, Ash, and all others, will be supplied of suitable age and size, and to any extent desired for nurseries, &c., at very moderate rates.

INDEX.

— — •◆• —

FRUIT DEPARTMENT.

ORNAMENTAL DEPARTMENT.

ESCULENT ROOTS.

www.ingramcontent.com/pod-product-compliance
Lightning Source LLC
Chambersburg PA
CBHW021536270326
41930CB00008B/1279